The Shape. of the Question

The Shape of the Question

THE MISSION OF THE CHURCH IN A SECULAR AGE

Kent S. Knutson

AUGSBURG PUBLISHING HOUSE
MINNEAPOLIS, MINNESOTA

THE SHAPE OF THE QUESTION

The Mission of the Church in a Secular Age

Manufactured in the United States of America

Contents

Preface

It can be argued that church presidents ought not to write books. In the first place, they could be doing more important things and second, they might say something which is different from what people think church presidents should say.

But it cannot be argued that church presidents ought not to think. Indeed, if they don't take time for reflection, they should seek other work. And if they think, they should be required to share their thoughts in one way or another.

I have taken the risk of sharing some of my thoughts. The mission of the church in this secular age is much on my mind. How shall the church evangelize? How shall it be true to the gospel in an unsettled and rebellious time?

This little book does not reveal all my thoughts, nor does it speak to every facet of how to be the church in this generation. But it attempts to begin a little dialog.

Nor is it intended to interest everyone. This book assumes a considerable amount of theological knowledge which, I am happy to say, is in the Christian community.

If you do not understand what I am saying, that is my fault, not yours. If you disagree with what is said, one or both of us may either be at fault or need further conversation.

It is my prayer that Jesus Christ, my Lord, is here glorified, and his body, the church, made more aware of its mission.

A Little Excursus

There are at least two kinds of people in the world. There are those who prefer questions and those who prefer answers.

Let me illustrate. Some years ago, when our children were much younger, we read at evening devotions that part of the Gospel of John which includes the sentence, "No one has seen God at any time." The ensuing conversation was not on the program.

One son (eight at the time) burst forth with a series of questions. How can that be? Isn't Jesus God?

Doesn't the Bible tell us about Jesus? Didn't people see Jesus? Why does the Bible first tell us that Jesus is God and then that no one has seen God? He was a question lover. His mind was revealed by the questions he asked.

A daughter, wiser because she was two years older, felt called upon to answer. For her, questions were unsettling. Life was not made up of questions but of answers. Every question deserved a complete and happy answer so one could get on with the business of doing things rather than thinking.

Her answer was a ten year level explanation of the incarnation: "Yes, he was God and man, but one did not see God when one saw Jesus because he was a man, so the Bible was right on both counts." But her answer did not satisfy her brother, for his mind was on the questions at that moment and not answers. He burst out with his real question, "How do we know they didn't make the whole thing up?"

That stopped the conversation. But it made possible some wonderful conversations when the lights were out before sleep and the reflective powers are sometimes good and unhurried. It is doubtful that these good learning experiences would ever had occurred without the hard question being asked.

Questions are interesting. Some questions do not have full and clear answers. They lead to partial answers which lead to other questions and other answers and the process is called learning. But they are dangerous if they remain only questions.

Answers are interesting. They are the stakes by which one nails down the tent of life. But they are dangerous if they cut the mind off from learning or if they do not lead to commitment and action.

We are, I suppose, at different times, all question lovers and answer lovers.

The really important matter is to want to ask the right questions so one is forced to search for the right answers. It is not wrong to reflect on the question itself. Is it the right question? Is it asked properly? What kind of presuppositions does the question itself reveal? Some questions are in themselves answers for they tell us something about ourselves.

This little book asks some questions, some that we ask ourselves and some that others ask.

The question of the mission of the church is a big question. It requires many sorts of answers—and it requires some additional questions about the age in which the church seeks to serve.

The mission of the church is clear in any age. It is to proclaim and live the gospel of our Lord Jesus Christ. Therefore it must understand that gospel, and it must know how to proclaim it so men can hear, and it must seek the ways to live it.

I believe the faith is being challenged in a particular way today. We must ask why. I believe the church is not altogether clear about the ways to proclaim and live the gospel. What are the particular problems of communication? What are the particular tasks to be accomplished?

This big question cannot be answered in one book. But its shape can be examined.

1

The Question
of the Age

The mission of the church encounters many problems today: declining rural populations, massive growth and problems in the urban situation, a warped economy, racial tension, poverty, international disorder and population problems of a kind that affect the whole world. But the chief problem, one which is the most dangerous and perhaps the most fruitful for us, is a rather strange and vague thing called secularism. I should like to speak in rather subtle and sometimes perhaps difficult terms about something called the shape of the question.

The Great Debate About God

Historians will probably look back on our time and call it "The Great Debate About God." This debate engulfs the whole theological spectrum from the radical fringes of the "God is Dead" movement on the one hand to the *avant-garde* Roman Catholics on the other. It is a public debate which receives continuing comment in the newspapers as well as in theological journals and thus involves the man on the street as well as the theologian in his study.

Why this kind of debate at this particular time? The question about God is not a new question. It was a question that Moses asked when in that desert he asked, "What is your name, God?" and received that strange and wonderful answer, "I am that I am." It was Paul's question when he gave that speech on the Areopagus in the middle of Greek culture and talked to the Greeks about their monument to the unknown God. The problem of articulating a language about God has never been very far from us but the shape of the question in our day has assumed proportions and characteristics and an intensity that seems to be more critical and perhaps more hopeful than at any time since the Reformation.

It is possible of course to think about the present situation as being somewhat faddish. Theological research and comment has swept across the sky like a searchlight, paused for a moment on an interesting object, and will soon move on to other concerns. In past Christian history the church concentrated from time to time on particular aspects of its faith. The church spent about six or seven centuries of its early

history interpreting and evaluating its Christology—
its understanding of the Christ. During the Middle
Ages the doctrine of God was the dominant theme
but that was somewhat swept aside by the Reformation which concentrated on the doctrine of salvation.
So the church has chosen to evaluate its faith at different periods in history. It may be that at this time in
history the church is being forced to look at one of
its basic tenets of faith by the society which is around
it. I believe that is the case.

From all indications we have entered into an era
of change in man's dealing with the question of God.
At the heart of this question is the emergence of the
secular man. The fruit of Copernicus and Darwin has
ripened on the tree. Western man has a different
understanding of himself and his world than did the
generations which went before him. Man in this age
feels that he belongs to this age, this saeculum, this
generation. He is concerned with this life, with the
here and now. He is this-worldly, some would say
who like that language, as opposed to other-worldly.
He affirms the temporal character of his existence and
finds the other-worldly meaningless. Knowledge is
understood to be that which is gained by human
endeavor and is based on the exercise of man's ra-
tional faculties and his powers of observation alone.
Theology has doubtful credentials and belongs to the
realm of the emotional, the poetical, and the illusory.

This is another way of saying that man has become autonomous, that is, he has become self-initiating, self-establishing, and self-understanding. If he is a thorough-going secularist, his autonomy is complete: there is no higher being than himself. Man must create his own values, set his own standards and goals, and work out his own salvation. Nothing transcends man's own powers and intelligence. What is important in trying to identify the secular man is not what he says but what he does. Many people who use the name of God are really practical atheists because their naming of God has no influence on anything they think or do. They have become dishonest secularists and our churches are full of them.

Secular man may be the way he is because of the technological era in which we live. Heidegger says that what is dangerous about our situation today is that our present intellectual equipment is inadequate to cope with a technological world. The metaphysics which has served us hitherto, whether materialistic or idealistic or Christian, is incapable of closing the gap between us and the fateful advent of this era of technology.

This man, this truly secular man, is characterized by a rigorous honesty and energy. He still asks questions because it is the nature of man to ask questions and he probably still asks the right questions. At the root of his attitude is the basic cry "Wherein lies meaning?" It is an epistemological question, that is, it is a question which arises out of a desire to know *how to know*. How can we know the truth? Pilate's question is still being raised today. And the traditional answer which has been given in Western civilization—God—brings another question. What do you mean by that? Tell us, what does the word God mean? This really is a Lutheran question occurring at key points in Luther's catechism. What does this mean for us, not just what does it say, but what does it mean? How shall it be interpreted? How shall it be applied?

What does this mean? is a very difficult question to answer for at least two reasons. First, because secular man has fallen into a trap in the way that he understands the question. It is possible to ask a question in such a way as to already determine the answer. It is possible to ask a question in such a way that no answer is expected. It is possible to ask a question in such a way as to require the one who seeks the answer to ask another question: What do you mean by the question? Asking a question does not in and of itself always permit an answer. It depends on the kind of question, the purpose of the question, the context out of which the question comes. Sometimes a question only deserves another question. Secular man, I believe, has asked this question out of a particular cultural commitment that is a trap for him and no kind of answer in and of itself will satisfy him. The second difficulty is that those who claim to believe in God have not paid enough attention to this question to know how to handle an answer. We have not had the theological perception or the interest or the intellectual equipment to be able to deal with that question. So we have created a confrontation which is a deadlock.

One concern is the question itself and how the question arises. Another is about the philosophical roots of the situation. It is my opinion that one can understand this problem by examining two philosophical commitments to the question, "Wherein lies meaning?"

The first school is Existentialism. It means simply preoccupation with one's own existence. It is not a typically American point of view. It comes to us from Europe where it made considerable inroads into the theological world, especially into New Testament studies, and is currently making its way into American life, especially in the arts—in films, in novels, and other forms of art that affect our culture so much, such as television.

The second school is Analytic Philosophy or philosophy of analysis, which is a dominant view, I believe, in our society. A product of the Anglo-Saxon culture, that is, a heritage of England and her philosophical history, it is characteristic of that age of the rise of modern science of which we are such an intimate part. We must try to understand what this means for the stance and growth of American culture.

Existentialism

Existentialism is not a new idea in the history of man. It goes back to Socrates, the ancient Greek philosopher whose dictum was "Know Thyself." Through the history of philosophical thought it has been articulated again and again by some of the great thinkers of the Western world: Augustine, the great theologian of the early church; Pascal, in the very late Middle Ages; and Kierkegaard, Danish Lutheran philosopher of the last century. It has been an especially interesting point of view in the development of Reformation theology. Luther had a strong dash of it himself. The Small Catechism is the best way of getting at Luther's fundamental thought. The first article says, "I believe in God the Father Almighty, Maker of Heaven and Earth" and the question comes, "What does this mean?" What does it mean that we say that God has created all of the universe? Luther's answer is, "I believe that God has created *me*." That's what it means! To say that God created all of the universe means to *me* that he created *me*.

In our time, the kind of existentialism we are confronted with has become so pristine, so perfect, so radical in its application, so closely and carefully defined as to make it almost impossible to answer the question, what does God mean? This new brand of existentialism assumes that man lives at best in a neutral world and at worst in a hostile world. The source of meaning does not come from the world, not from anything that one knows about the world around him, not from his environment, not from the earth, not from any kind of examination of history, but comes from within the self.

"I know the world," says the existentialist, "when I know myself. When I know myself, then I am able to understand and know everything that there is to know about the whole world." Man, says the existentialist, is aware that he is aware. He knows that he is. The world is not aware. There is therefore an infinite gulf between a living creature and his existence and other kinds of reality.

Man can search for meaning only within his own realm of consciousness. No meaning comes from a world which is not aware. You cannot derive truth from something which does not have the possibility of consciousness. Truth is a name only for knowing and knowing is an activity which can be done only by one who is aware that he is aware. The world's reality to an existentialist is something which occurs within his consciousness. The stars, the trees, the smell of fall and the smell of rain, the fog and the sun, all these things may exist outside one's own consciousness but they become real only within one's own consciousness. Those things are real only to you and to you only insofar as you experience them. So the self is not a point of non-dimension as Decartes had said, despite the fact that most of the Western world has thought like that.

One of the strange things about the intelligent man today is that he has not stopped to think about what he is. He has not stopped to think about what mind is. The existentialist has tried to rectify that, trying to say to Western man, "You have never stopped to evaluate and understand *your* existence. You have spent these hundreds of years evaluating only what the world is like. You have examined the world. You have not come to an awareness really of what you are yourself." So they say, "What are you?" And the answer comes—you are a *Dasein,* a *being there.* You are something thrown into the world, you are real, you exist, you are something in yourself. You are not something by virtue of the fact that you are in the world or by virtue of the fact that you are related to something else, or by virtue of the fact that somebody made you what you are. You are what you are because you are there. You must begin from that point, accepting the fact that you are there and that you are aware that you are there.

Part of your awareness, part of the texture of your

existence, includes what is called the power of dis-closedness. Meaning is disclosed within you. You have the power not only to be aware that you are aware but you have the power to learn. You are able to discover, you are able to conceptualize, you are able to have a revelation to use theological language. This *Dasein,* this being there, this existence is the place where reality is to be found. *That's* what is *real. You* are real. Your awareness is real, your power of de-cision and disclosedness is genuine reality.

This disclosedness, this revelation, this discovery that you have as part of your own nature tells you that you *care.* You care about your own existence, you care who you are, you care whether you're afraid or glad, you care what other people think, you care whether you are loved or hated, you care what each day is going to be like. And that which threatens you most, that which is the thing you care most about is a strange, abstract thing called *nothingness.* For if the chief reality to you is yourself, your being there, your existence, then that which you care most about would be the threat that you are not. And if it is true that in every existence of man there is this power of dis-closedness, there is also in every man the fear of death. It is the given anxiety of every man's existence. And therefore he is not only a being who cares but he is a being who is anxious, and he knows that whatever he is to be, he must handle it himself. He must decide, he must shape it, he must understand his situation.

Several possibilities are open to this kind of thinker. It may be that there is no exit from this self, from this world, from this reality. Jean Paul Sartre wrote a play called *No Exit*. Nothing lies outside the *Dasein* where meaning can be found. Whatever meaning there is must occur within man himself. That is man's freedom; that is also, of course, his threat. There is meaning, says Sartre, within the self, and this meaning is the experience in man's discovery of where meaning is and in his decision to assert freedom. For man can shake his fist against the world and say, "I don't care who you are and what you're like, how hostile and threatening you are to me, I assert myself and that's my freedom, that's where my meaning occurs."

Kierkegaard points out a second possibility. This self could also be made aware that it is a dependent self, that it lives over against its source of being. That is, that from which you came, that power out of which you issued, involves an awareness of your being dependent on that source. But this self discovery, he said, can be accomplished only by what he called an "existential leap" prompted by despair and grounded in nothing else than the grace of the One you are over against. That is, man does not only have within himself this power of discovery and awareness but he also has the power to receive a revelation of this awareness. It is only from the graciousness of the One out of which he comes that it is possible for man to discover his dependence and leap to that understanding. The name for this wholly other, this one infinitely qualitatively self-separated reality from man, yet the source of man is, in Kierkegaard's language, God. Now the difficulty with this view in the eyes of secular man is that it says nothing about this God. There is no content, no data, not even any language except the language of faith, the language of a man talking about God. There is no way to tell about the leap and no language that can convince another man of the leap but only a witness to the grace given for the leap.

In our generation we have been deeply affected by this way of looking at things. Modern psychiatry at least in some respects, is a case in point. The psychiatrist puts you on a couch and has you talk about yourself. Language becomes the entré into the self. He doesn't care what you did before he came, he doesn't care what you're going to do after you leave, he cares only what you *say,* he cares only about the expression of yourself, he cares only about what things mean to you. The emphasis here is on sincerity—the kind of faith which suggests that it only matters whether you believe in yourself—an emphasis in much pastoral counseling today.

Analytic Philosophy

The second school is called Analytic Philosophy. It begins with the proposition that man is one of the entities in the world like other entities. Existentialism thought of man as being the center of his own universe and all the world being understood and seen within his consciousness. Your world is *the* world. But analytic philosophy thinks of you as one thing among a great many other things in the world. Everything in the world, including you, has its own reality. John Smith is one reality in a world of a hundred thousand million stars. "I know myself," he says, "when I know the world. When I have understood the world then I can begin to understand myself." The existentialist said that when I understand myself then I can understand the world. These are very different ways of thinking. Man has peculiar characteristics just as every reality has its own peculiar characteristics. But they are worldly characteristics, that is, they can be understood by understanding what the world is like. If you want to find out what a man is like you will have to find out what protein is like, what protons and electrons are like. You find out about the habits of animals. To understand what a man is like you understand first about the world because man is made out of that which the world is made of and when one understands the general laws of the universe, then one can say, "Well now, I understand what man is like." Meaning lies in the world itself, the empirical, the observable, the analyzable world at hand.

Analytic philosophy begins with the question of language. The existentialist also was very concerned about language as the expression of the self. The analytic philosopher thinks of language as the way man describes not himself, but the world. Language corresponds to the way the world is, it mirrors what is in the world. Everything is verified by examining the world to see whether it corresponds with the language which is used about the world.

Man, says this point of view, has often been misled by irrelevant and illusory questions. A clarification of what man is saying is needed before we can see what meaning is. If the question is, what is meaning, then we have to look at the language men are using to see whether they are actually saying correct things or whether they are being misled by their own language. By examining the world and then examining man's language in relation to the world you can discover meaning.

What does it mean when anyone says God? What is the reference for God? Where in the world is God? The point is that according to analytic philosophy language is the key. Everybody wants to know whether something is really real. He wants to be shown. He He wants to know what the facts are. Even people interested in believing in God with as much sincerity and experience and hope and love as they can muster nevertheless want their religion undergirded by some kind of facts. They want it to be established whether or not the whale swallowed Jonah, whether or not God created the world in six days. If God did not create the world in six days, there is something wrong with the whole system and God himself is brought into question because he has not yet been proved! Everything must be proved because that's what truth is, that's what meaning is. Meaning is something not to be discovered within the self, but by an examination of the world.

As man accumulates more and more knowledge about the world more and more questions are answered, the day will arrive when there are no questions left. The question of man's own existence, the question of death, the questions which gnaw away at man inside, will all disappear. They will no longer exist. The riddles will vanish, concludes the secular man. They are the kinds of questions for which there are no answers because the question was based on a wrong understanding of what meaning is.

The Christian Response to the Secular Man

What has been the reaction of the Christian community to this kind of world in which we have lived and in which we are emerging more and more clearly? For a very long period the response of the Christian community to the rise of secular man and his philosophical heroes was listless and non-productive. In a way we have just lived through what I call a very biased anti-philosophical period. Oscar Cullmann, a respected professor of New Testament is a typical example. He considers every philosophical question either dangerous or stupid. Karl Barth took the other path of carefully examining philosophical questions and it took him a lifetime because he examined every philosophical question. When he had done it all he decided it wasn't of any value. Paul Tillich was a rather lonely voice who insisted that such questions be taken seriously, that somehow one had to become involved because they were the cry of modern man, or in his view, of the men of all times. And he said the answers were to be found in the Christian faith.

These men are really of a past generation in many ways. We have no great theological heroes or leaders in our day. We have to grapple with these things as a Christian community if we are interested in the mission of the church, for the mission of the church forces us to raise these questions. What is the context into which the Word is to be spoken? There have been some responses to the question of meaning and how we can speak of God.

One of the early responses was to say that God is

inexpressible. That is, the domain and character of the religious faith is such that the faith cannot be expressed or communicated in any way demanded by the question. This, to me, is a very unsatisfactory answer. If God is completely inexpressible Christianity becomes a mystical religion where you can think but not talk. I would have to agree with the analytic philosopher Wittgenstein who said in a very pithy little sentence: "Whereof one cannot speak, thereof one must be silent." If you can't say it, don't say it. And the people who have been saying that God is inexpressible have been talking about God and just as they themselves would have to admit, it never made any sense. One has no idea of whether what one believes or thinks is illusion or reality unless one is able to talk about it.

Another response has been that the faith is irrational—it can be spoken about and talked about, but it doesn't make sense when you do it. It's a kind of secret language, only for the initiated. It has no content, but is a kind of liturgical language. Christians can talk about God and it means something to each one of them, not because of what is said, but because what is said does communicate something about what is believed and thought. So you cannot examine the language to find out what God is like but you can hear Christians talking to one another and say, "Well, something is going on there that they understand and know about but no one on the outside can know about it." Faith, says one of these writers is a "blik," that is, man has been seized by a point of view, by a certain kind of power and he believes despite himself, but what he says about his believing is really irrational. And this does not impress secular man. It seems to answer the question, wherein lies meaning, by a sort of agnosticism. Man lives as *if* something were true but he does not really know.

I'm afraid some of this kind of agnosticism can be found in church and among the clergy. A bright confirmation student comes to the pastor and says, "Why does the church teach this?" and the pastor, perhaps not knowing or not being able to handle it, or being threatened by the brightness of this confirmation student says, "Well, you can't talk about that, you can only believe it." It can't be understood, it has to be believed. There is *something* to that answer, of course. Yet I cannot believe that faith in and of itself is something irrational.

Thirdly, there have been some new ideas. Some just pick up the gospel of Existentialism and say, "We've got to run with this one." This *is* a view of reality which is possible for the Christian faith to use. The Christian faith can be explained in these categories. we can learn how the ancient church dealt with problems like this and it is quite possible that in speaking for the church today we will say, "Let us take this point of view and see if we can communicate the Christian faith to people who think this way." Schubert Ogden, for example, says that man is aware of more than his awareness, that his disclosedness within himself is a direct illumination of the source of his being. That is, every man knows God. Some Roman Catholics have been using the term "anonymous God," which means the knowledge of God that is built into the very nature of man. Man must be made aware of this built-in knowledge of God, and the one who does this is Jesus of Nazareth. When we meet Jesus we see in him something of what God is like and thus we recognize that we know God.

Others also speak in this vein. Helmut Gollwitzer of Germany is one. Gerhard Ebeling of Switzerland in his worldly language about God is trying to do this. Ian Ramsey of England suggests that the language Christians should use to communicate the faith and their meaning of God is an odd language, and is deliberately different from the language of the world. Not based on an empirical knowledge of history it creates discernment and commitment in men. There is a self-authenticating power in language.

Others are saying, "No, let's take analytical philosophy and build on that." John Hick suggests that it is possible to talk about the verifiability of Christianity and of God. He calls the faith "eschatologically verifiable," that is, it is verified in the future, therefore it can be talked about. The analytical philosopher agrees that it is meaningful to talk about God if the Christian can show that even though he is not verifiable at the moment for one reason or another (we don't yet have the best instruments, the time isn't right, and other reasons), but he is verifiable in the future. Then we have achieved a common ground for discussion and perhaps there is some kind of relationship between the thoroughly modern secular man and the Christian, so that becomes possible to have meaningful discourse about God.

Hick tells a little story called "The Parable of the Celestial City." Two men are walking along a road and one man says to the other, "Over the hill and at the end of this road is a celestial city." The other man replies, "No, there is no celestial city." These two men walk along the same road, see the same world, have available the same knowledge, have no secrets from each other. Each agrees with the other that the world they see is the same world. One is not smarter than the other, or more honest, but one says there is a celestial city and the other says there is not. What do men do about that? According to Hick, they walk together on the road, they love one another, they help one another, but not until they go around the corner and over the hill will they know whether or not there is a celestial city. But it is verifiable. The presence of God is a future prospect for man and men must live side by side with different hopes until that day—one with faith and the other without. But the man who does not have the hope knows that the claim of the other man is a true claim because he admits that it is verifiable.

Some say that we do not yet have the ability to speak to this question, that we live in a particular age when we must be quiet. But we are on the edge of a new age in which the language of God will become completely re-formed and made more powerful than ever before. However, we must be modest and must wait for that.

And finally there are those, but very few I would hope, who say we can never speak of God at all. For the word *God* has no function any longer and there is no referent. We must cling to Jesus himself only and redefine God in terms of the life of this man, Jesus of Nazareth. One can speak about God only in terms of his demise. There is no God, it was said rather facetiously, and Jesus is his son. In some ways, this is what is behind the Jesus movement today. The fascination with Jesus of Nazareth, with no real understanding or language to speak about the transcendent, is an outgrowth of this philosophy.

It is my conviction that we live in a time when these kinds of theological and philosophical questions must be faced by the church if it is to be responsible in its mission.

Henri D. Lubac, a French philosopher, said, "Industrial civilizations are by their nature atheist in character as agricultural civilizations are pagan, (that is, urban civilizations have no gods, agricultural civilizations are pagan, that is, they have many gods). Faith in the true God is quite unaffected by this, but as they become increasingly profane modern civilizations do face us with the danger of losing God, yet maybe they will give us the opportunity to discover him in greater depth. This discovery could pave the way for new syntheses while doing away once and for all with the effects of our primitive confusion."

In his film, "The Silence," Ingmar Bergman tells the story of two sisters traveling in a foreign country. Neither one knows the language. To make matters worse, they are estranged from each other, so they don't really talk to each other. When one of the sisters becomes ill, they are forced to stay in this country. The story is about the silence—a world without language. The one sister becomes so depressed that she turns inward and becomes emotionally ill. The other turns outward from herself, insists on contacts with the world and turns to a life of promiscuity because she must have contact with another person. To be human is to be spoken to. A silent world, a world without meaning, threatens to extinguish man. There is a word, says the Christian. There is a word to break the silence and to speak to man in this time. His name is Jesus Christ.

2

The Question
of the Power of God

We are not accustomed to talk about power in the church. We talk about relationships, redemption, grace, Christ, the sacraments, the Word of God, but the word power is not part of our theological vocabulary. And yet we exercise power all the time in our daily lives. There are power structures in every human community, in every academic community, every congregation. Power structures constitute one way for human beings to relate themselves to one another and to deal with one another.

What is the power God gives to us? We need to look at the question of power from a number of different perspectives so we can understand how power relates to theology, faith, and life.

The original Greek of the New Testament uses two words for power. One word is *dynamis,* the word from which our word dynamite is derived. It means that kind of power which is possessed—potential power, power which is latent and waiting to be used, such as dynamite. Dynamite looks innocent. It doesn't look powerful, but it has potential power, power not yet released but present. The other Greek word is *exousia,* the kind of power which is being expressed—expressive power, articulated power, acted-out power.

The Power of God

The power of God can be talked about in different ways. One is the creative power of God, *exousia* power. And that which he created, that universe which is a result of this *exousia* is itself a power. The world is understood in Scripture not in terms of its inertness, not in terms of its weight or its size, not in terms of space it occupies, but it is understood as a pulsating, moving, changing reality whose every moment is related to and dependent on God's power. Most adults have been trained in a school system operating with the philosophy that goes back to Sir Isaac Newton. That philosophy describes the world in terms of its mathematics, in terms of its weight and size. We have thought of the earth as something inert, something that can be measured, something that follows certain rules and laws. The Bible, however, provides a different thought world. The Bible thinks of the world in terms of history, of movement, of change, of growth, and direction, in terms of pursuit for a goal. The universe in which we live and which surrounds us is a power.

In his creative act God brought structure and order out of chaos. The world was chaotic, says Genesis, and God brought about a purpose, a goal; he brought about a meaning where there had been no meaning before. And one of the aspects of this order is justice. God brought about justice and this universe requires proper ends, proper goals, and proper relationships to establish the order God wishes for his universe.

The word *power* is also used in the Bible to describe Christ's work. The work of redemption is a power. I believe that in the Lutheran tradition we ought to understand the work of Christ in terms of its power as well as in other terms. We should understand that Christ's work was a battle against powers and the whole life of Jesus is shown as a life pitted against evil—against all that injures and hurts mankind. The work of Christ is seen in the midst of conflict. In fact life among men is pictured in the New Testament as the life which is full of conflict. The rebellious forces of evil in the world were taken on by our Lord and defeated.

Life is an experience in which good and evil are in constant confrontation and we cannot expect anything less than that. It is not God's intention that life should be so serene, so without challenge or conflict that man never achieves his full potential. Jesus is not pictured as a placid, sentimental, and retiring person who sometimes gives himself over to other powers and by virtue of that weakness becomes a savior. He is rather pictured as a warrior, as the fighter, as the one who overcomes—the one who accomplishes through weakness yet one who accomplishes by strength. The work of Christ is that of a leader of a great army. The death of Christ is not humiliation but victory and it is victory which promises freedom for man. St. Paul and St. John many times express such promises: "You shall know the truth and the truth shall make you free." "If the Son makes you free you will be free indeed, for freedom Christ has set us free." Luther picks up this theme in his explanation to the Second Article: "I know that Jesus Christ, true God begotten of the Father from eternity and also true man born of the Virgin Mary is my Lord who bought and freed me from sin, death, and the power of the devil."

The resurrection of our Lord is understood by the New Testament as an expression of the power of God. The resurrection of Jesus is not only that of the coming to life of a dead man. It is that, but more. Jesus of Nazareth who died and was put into the tomb was made alive again by God. But it isn't his coming to life again as Jesus of Nazareth. It is rather his exaltation to Lordship, his exaltation to be the ruler of the universe. The risen Lord is not in the same state of reality as Jesus of Nazareth. He has become one beyond time and beyond space. He is no longer the weakling, he is no longer the Jew of Palestine, but he is the one God made Lord and King who rules all things, the past and the future that awaits us.

The doctrine of the Holy Spirit in the New Testament is a doctrine that deals with power. At Pentecost the message was given, "You will be filled with power," and the gift of the Holy Spirit is a gift of power we celebrate in Baptism and in the Lord's Supper. God has not only told us that he already has won the victory and that his power is in the power of the universe, but he has also said that his power is given to us, his power is present in us in the church and in our inner selves.

In the Christian tradition we have pulled these various ideas together in the phrase, "Word of God." We use that phrase in different ways and for different reasons. When the pastor preaches we say he is preaching the Word of God. When one Christian by an act of love to another person shows his understanding of the Gospel we can say that he is communicating the Word of God. We say the Law is the Word of God and that the Gospel is the Word of God. We say the Bible is the Word of God.

We have not always understood how the phrase "Word of God" relates to the idea of power. God's

Word created the universe. God's Word was involved in the development of the people of Israel, the freeing of the slaves from Egypt, the prophetic voices who preached against social injustice. God's Word became flesh in the person of Jesus Christ. God's Word developed the earliest Christian community by the presence of the Spirit and the gathering together of the prophets and the apostles and the evangelists to interpret the events to give us still another word called the Bible. God's Word, God's power is exhibited among us in the preaching of the Word of that Bible. The Word also becomes a drama, an event given to us in our sacraments.

All of our theology is related to that phrase "Word of God." We say for example, that this Bible, this Word of God, has authority. The word authority is a translation of the Greek word *exousia,* a kind of power that exerts itself. The Bible is the Word of God not because men have been able to describe it by profound words and thereby made it powerful. It is the Word of God because that Word exerts a power which it possesses by its own nature. The power of the Bible is not in its perfection, not in its beauty, not in its historical accurateness. The Word of God is authority because it has a power which it possesses in and of itself, a power which it exerts. The Bible is the Word of God and exerts its own power in strange and wonderful ways, in ways we do not expect, and at times when we do not want it. Yet God controls that Word and it is his Word because he has made it his Word.

If you want to find out what the Bible is like, you have to study it. You cannot find out about the Bible by just talking about how it ought to be. You find out about it by studying it and learning from it and discovering for yourself what it is. Sometimes when we do that we are surprised. We may find that the Bible is not the way our grandmothers thought it was. We may discover that it is not the way we used to think it was. We may learn that it is not always the way the pastor says it is. If we study it, make use of study helps, listening to others who have spent years in study, we may discover that it speaks in ways much richer and much more profound and uses methods quite different from what we had suspected or known. If God has chosen to speak through biblical witnesses who lived in their culture and in their time and spoke to communicate to us through *their* understanding of that time, then I shall have to accept it. If God chooses to speak through Balaam's ass, I shall have to accept that as his choice. God sometimes withholds things from me, he sometimes fans my curiosity and he sometimes makes me angry because he forces me to trust him and he will not submit himself to my demands as to how he ought to speak to me. He has his understanding of history, he chose the Jewish people for good reasons he has not altogether revealed to me.

And he spoke through long and tortured centuries until at last he spoke in and through his Son, Jesus Christ in a way that I can understand and that will engender my love.

And because of this I know the Bible is inspired—God-breathed. It means the Bible has power to speak what God wishes to have spoken and it speaks that no matter what form the Bible is in. I find it strange when people tell me the Bible must be this way or that way because it is inspired, that because it is inspired they know who wrote a certain book in the Bible or how many animals went into the ark. The inspiration of the Bible has nothing to do with such questions. However many animals there were in the ark, or whoever wrote the Book of Hebrews or the Letter to the Colossians, they are inspired. God speaks in his word. His *dynamis* explodes and becomes *exousia*. The perfection of the Bible is not related to its inspiration. The Bible is what it is because of its power.

The same thing can be said about preaching. A sermon may be powerful even if it has grammatical errors and even if it has the wrong number of points. The size of the bread you receive at the Lord's Supper or the kind of water in Baptism has nothing to do with effectiveness, for the power does not rely on the form through which it comes. It is God's Word, said Luther, which is the power in Baptism and not the water and it is not man's understanding which makes the Bible what it is, but what God has made it and he has made it his authority, his power. The Word of God is a name for the means by which God's power comes to us.

The Power of the Church

And what now of the church's power? Two major aspects of this subject must be emphasized—personal power and corporate power.

Personal power is a name for that creative potential power God has given every man—the power of reason, the power of creative imagination, the power of reproduction, the power to organize, the power to analyze and criticize, the power to make decisions. Every family on earth, says Paul, is related to God's name and that means related to his power. Therefore we respect every other man and find ourselves responsible to cooperate with all other men and learn from all other men because God has given the power of creaturehood to every man.

In our tradition we may have misunderstood some of our great and profound ideas. We have taken a phrase such as "total depravity" and interpreted it to mean that man does not have power. But total depravity means that no man has the power to save himself. It was not meant to say that man does not possess power. Man does possess power to be used for justice, for good in the world, for creating and sustaining and designing and organizing and God expects man to use that power. The Reformation theology did not mean to say that man ought to be deprived of his potential for making this earth a good place to live. In fact, God expects men to use their power to do this.

God also gives to men the power that makes them whole again, that restores their personhood and their creaturehood—the power of salvation. He gives to men the power to be free, the power to exhibit love, the power to be patient, the power to enjoy. Man lives in a world where he still participates in sin and conflict, but he has been given the power to exist in this kind of world. He lives in the hope and in the certitude that God has given him the power of salvation, that these evil conflicts will not endure, that they will not be the final victors. That has been guaranteed by the work of Christ.

The most powerful gift that God gives man is the power of confidence, the power of faith, the power to trust, the power to overcome the depression and the limitations of life in a world with so much conflict and so much evil. And God expects us to utilize these powers so that life for mankind becomes much better than it is when men refuse to take on themselves the responsibility for the good of all mankind.

There is also *corporate power*—the power of the church. The church is a community, a reality in itself.

It is the body of Christ, says St. Paul, it is Christ's presence in history. Like the Word of God which is the form through which God's power comes, so the church, the body of Christ, is also a form through which God's power comes. It is not just a collection of human powers. It is not only a volunteer society as sociologists and perhaps some theologians may want to say. The church is a reality God has created, a reality greater than the collection of the individuals who are in it.

The church is a reality in which you believe. I believe in the Holy Christian Church, we confess in the Creed. It is something we can trust because it is something greater than ourselves, something that has enveloped us, grasped us, lifted us up and placed us in a new order of being.

The church exhibits power in several ways. It exhibits ethical power. God has given to the church the task to be the witness to the justice he had in mind when he created the whole world. The church is to be a conscience, for God intended the creation of life to be one of order and of justice. The church is not to be the only conscience. Other people are wise and other men also have personal power. Others may be wiser than we. They may love better than we do, and see things in society we are a little slow in seeing either because they are working harder at it, or because we are looking the other way, or because we haven't yet learned the wisdom God has made available to us. But God has given to us the power of justice and he asks us to exhibit it. He asks us to be open to the expression of ethical power.

In the past we have concentrated our ethical power more on individuals and on individual sins, such as adultery, lying, stealing, conceit, and jealousy. But there are also the corporate sins of society, the commitment to evil of a whole people. Ethical power is not just part of my personal power but is also part of the corporate nature of the church itself.

The church also has sociological power. We are a community in a society. We are the majority in this nation. We are a greater power than General Motors if we really exert it. We are a greater power than any one of the political parties. We are a greater power than any of the power blocs in the racial groups or the cultural groups *if* the Christian community asserts itself. If it acted as a Christian community it would simply by virtue of its thinking, voting, doing, teaching, acting in this society have a tremendous power in this nation and in the world. There is a sociological power simply by being what we are. We are rapidly losing that kind of power in this society. Yet we must recognize that the Christian community in society is a power and we need to learn how to manage that power.

We do that through a third dimension called political power, a power God gives his church. And about this we know very little. We are naive and we have made many mistakes in the church. But there come critical moments in history, when the church must exert its power, when it must be *exousia,* when the power which is its potential must come alive and express itself in society. We can do this in three steps.

First of all, we need to clarify for ourselves the nature of the problems of evil. We have begun to understand that there is corporate sin as well as individual sin. It is also important to clarify what needs to be accomplished in this society to exert this kind of power. We must take seriously the task of educating ourselves.

In the second place, we as a church need to learn the art of participation in society so we understand the effect of evil and injustice in the society. This we have not known too well because as a community we have been so acculturated, so bound by the limitations of our experience as white middle class people, mostly of a cultural European heritage that we have not understood how other people think, hurt, and live. The church in our time is sent to go out from itself into the world to preach and be the gospel in other places. A mission church, one that is sent, is not one that stays in one place and brings the world to it but a community that worships and learns together and then goes out. We must learn the art of participation so we are able to understand the context where the Gospel is to be preached and lived.

In the third place, we remember that at some times the church must express political power. In many ways our own church body has been a passive church, lacking in self-confidence, not trusting in God's power, and not altogether willing to speak against evil in the public realm. There have been some brilliant moments in the church. When Norway was occupied by Hitler's Nazis in World War II, the church arose and said clearly to the invading forces: NO. It acted with conviction. It became a power in that place and at that time against evil political forces arrayed against it. Yet at other times the church has not done that. We need to reflect on our task and on the power God gives this church so that we may be prepared for times that call for a clear prophetic witness. We cannot silently watch the genocide of another race. We cannot permit one nation's power to control the world to such an extent that the majority of the world suffers because of the arrogance or the power of that one nation. And if we are able to speak then we have the right and the responsibility so to do.

3

The Question
of the Christ
of Tradition

Christology is the doctrine of the person of Jesus
Christ. In the traditional teaching of systematic theology, Christology is dealt with before Soteriology, the
doctrine of the work of Christ. This is logically de-
fensible, but it is a different order from that of the
New Testament. Here men were confronted *first* by
the history of the words and actions of a man, Jesus of
Nazareth, and they responded to it by a confession of
faith as to who he was. Christology as we know it
grows out of the reflection of faith of the post-scriptur-
al church in response to the totality of the scriptural
witness and is deeply embedded in the understanding
of what tools and experiences best interpret and communicate that response.

The church spent its first six centuries in discussion

and controversy concerning the language and the categories that should be used to conceptualize and safeguard the faith. It is out of this period that "classical" or "ecumenical" or "Chalcedonian" Christology became dogma and passed into the universal tradition of the church. The three ecumenical creeds, essentially Christological in concern and nature, are the legacy of this great period of reflection and decision. The Council of Chalcedon in 451 is the high water mark of this development and became the permanent contribution, although challenges and interpretations continued until at least 680-81 and the Sixth Ecumenical Council at Constantinople. Hence the name "Chalcedonian" or "classical" Christology.

The Impulses Which Created the Controversies

The development of classical Christology did not occur in a vacuum but came about by virtue of specific situations and problems, indeed, profound crises.

First, the character of the biblical witness itself called for such a response. The New Testament contains 27 books which exhibit both an intense unity and a wide diversity. Written by different men at different times with somewhat different goals, they use a variety of vocabularies, perspectives, and historical data. A rather clear line of development occurs within this corpus. Words change their meaning, new areas of concern arise, others drop out, and there is a general mushrooming of understanding as that community, led by the Spirit, considers its understanding of the Christ. Christology was a developing response to the total encounter with the Christ, not only to his human and earthly history, but also to his resurrected and exalted Lordship over the church, even in the writing of the New Testament. This development did not stop with the formulation of the canon. Christians needed and wanted a *focus* by which the unity of the New Testament witness could be preserved without destroying the richness of its variety. A cohesive confession of faith was deeply desired. This required, in their judgment, confessions or creeds by which the faith of the New Testament could be summarized.

Second, the church of those first centuries was engaged in a program of mission whose essential ingredient was the communication of a Hebraic faith to a Greek culture. Could the faith be restated or interpreted via the categories by which men understand themselves and the world? Can there be *any* meaning without communication through the concepts in which meaning is believed to reside?

Third, the Christians themselves lived in a rather sophisticated intellectual climate and desired understanding for themselves. They needed answers to their own questions, questions which had not occurred to the bliblical writers or were not germane to the Hebraic approach to reality. Basically they asked, how shall we understand "The Word became flesh"?

Fourth, a fierce internal struggle developed in the church which required clarification and, if possible, resolution. Two broad commitments to the "methodology of meaning" were pressing. One was Ebionitism (meaning "the poor"). This grew out of a Jewish understanding regarding the integrity of man. If Jesus Christ is to be understood in terms of who he is, one must begin with his humanity, with his history. This is the given, the assured. His divinity must be derived from and expressed in the categories of human existence. The second was Docetism (from the Greek word which means "to seem") which derived from the "Greek" view that reality (and therefore meaning) lies in the unseen and the eternal, that is, in God. One must begin with the divine and see the earthly or human only in terms of the divine initiative and nature.

These two beginning points clashed. When Ebionitism became too pre-occupied with the humanity of Christ, it did not manage to relate the divine to Christ at all, thus becoming in the eyes of the church a heresy, that is, a teaching so extreme it distorted the gospel. This view had a number of schools and opinions and learnings. One of the most prominent was "adoptionism," the idea that God was related to Christ in any special sense only temporarily, for example, from his baptism until his cry from the cross, "My God, my God, why hast Thou forsaken me"? The later philosophical slogan, "The finite is not capable of the infinite" is a descendant of this view.

When Docetism, as it most often did, became too pre-occupied with the divinity of Christ, it did not manage to pay sufficient attention to his humanity and thus became heretical. This, too, had its varieties and influences. Docetism remains a pervasive and powerfully subtle influence and, is as dangerous as the ebionitic spirit of our time.

These two basic positions achieved high ecclesiastical prominence in theological schools in two ancient cities, Antioch and Alexandria, and there came about a clash between Antiochene (leaning toward the ebionitic) and Alexandrian (leaning toward the docetic) views.

The church was not a little bewildered. How should it find its way? The solution is the story of classical Christology.

The Questions of Classical Christology

The church sought to deal with three basic questions:

1) In what sense do we call Jesus human?

2) In what sense do we call Jesus divine?

3) Assuming answers to the first two questions, how are these two, humanity and divinity, related to one another in one person?

It must be remembered that the way one puts a question and the questions one chooses to answer influences the answers. Further the method by which one seeks answers plays an important role.

First, note that the questions are asked without any apparent relation to the work of Christ, that is, to redemption. This was not intentionally neglected; indeed, it was their intention to safeguard redemption, but they did isolate these questions intellectually and thereby embarked on a dangerous enterprise. It wasn't until much later, the Reformation, in fact, that this was really noticed. They chose ontology (asking questions about being) rather than function (asking questions about deeds) as the area in which their understanding of the Christ would be located.

Second, they chose the categories of humanity and divinity, which are not explicit categories in the New Testament, but come from their own post-biblical cultural heritage. Thus they were answering very ultimate questions on the basis of *implicit* motifs in Scripture. They thought this was necessary because of their mission.

Third, they chose to answer these questions in almost wholly non-biblical language, that is, by using their own cultural vocabulary and concepts. This caused much discussion and bitterness mainly because they had no full consensus as to the meaning of the words they used. There was no final or perfect language to express the ideas agreed upon. They suffered from these problems even though they worked with the Greek language, the same language as the New Testament.

Fourth, they chose to deal primarily with the way the Gospel of John had seen the situation. The prologue to John uses the vocabulary of *word* or translated from the Greek, *logos*. This is not a customary use of language in the New Testament, let alone in the rest of John. Yet this seemed to those church fathers to be the best *entre* into the vast field of the human and the divine in Christ. "The Word became flesh" became *the* sentence for interpretation. The whole christological development can be said to be an answer to the question, "What does this mean?"

The Answers of Classical Christology

The answers that emerged out of this turmoil were clear, straight-forward, and, considering the nature of the questions, simple. They were for the faithful.

Question: In what sense do we call Jesus human?

Answer: In the full sense. In terms of his *being,* his *nature* that is, in terms of his being what he is, he is completely and fully and indeed truly human.

They had no real problem with this answer. The testimony of the New Testament is massive and explicit. He exhibited all the normal patterns of human behavior—anger, joy, sorrow, laughter, puzzlement, cleverness, discouragement, fatigue, hunger, evasiveness. He experienced all the great phases of human life—birth, growth, temptation, suffering, rejection, love, hope, death. He also was limited in space, in knowledge, in power, in his humanity. He was like us in everything.

Indeed he was the true man. He had all the aspects of humanity: will (this was hotly debated in the 7th century), soul, spirit, heart, mind, and whatever other words describe what man is.

He was not part man and part God. He was not only man in appearance and God internally. He was not a creature set apart from humanity in terms of his humanity (set apart in terms of a task is something else). In short, everything that a man is, Christ is.

This view is preserved for us especially in the Apostles' Creed and in all subsequent creeds. The creed we use did not achieve final form until the 8th century, but even the earliest form from the 2nd century carefully emphasized his human character—

who was born of the Holy Ghost and the Virgin
  Mary
who was crucified under Pontius Pilate
who was buried.

In terms of the actions of his humanity, great differences between the Christ and other men appeared. He did not sin and his deeds were redemptive for all men, but this was not the question. The question was, "Is he human?" The answer was, "yes." No modifications, adjustments, reservations, de-emphases, or slightings of this could be tolerated. Whatever man is, Jesus is a man.

Question: In what sense do we call Jesus divine?

Answer: In the full sense. In terms of his *being,* his *nature,* that is, in terms of his being what he is, he is completely and fully and truly divine.

This was a more difficult answer. The New Testament is very cautious about naming Christ God. The New Testament witness is almost always indirect and implicit and does not define proper categories for its interpretation. There is no defined category of divinity in the Scripture. To answer the question for themselves, the early fathers chose two tacks, both of which received their expression in the Nicene Creed first formulated in Nicea in 325 and then re-worked in the Council of Constantinople in 381.

First, they pinpointed the phrase *begotten, not made.*

The word *begotten* meant that Christ in his pre-existence (a most difficult word) was continuous with the Father in his being. This was in answer to the idea (called Arianism) that the Word which became flesh was not created by God at some point before the creation of the world but later than God's own generation(!) ("There was a time when God was not").

They did not answer the question of his relation to the Father in terms of his obedience. (That was not the question). The New Testament clearly talks about Jesus being subject to the Father. This idea could remain as far as this discussion was concerned, but he shared the Father's eternal origin *in his divine essence*.

Second, they coined the phrase (actually the suggestion came from a layman, the Emperor Constantine, whose theological sophistication was not noteworthy)

Of one substance with the father.

The great (or notorious) word was *substance*. Simply put, substance meant the power to persist or the power to continue to be what it is. They said whatever it is that makes God what he is, that Jesus Christ shares fully. The beauty of this word was that it did not require a full understanding of *what* God's substance is. It was a way by which the divinity of Christ could be conceptualized without impairing the mystery.

The argument was over *similar substance* or *same substance*. Was he like God in his being or did he share God's own being. The answer was the latter without equivocation. He was like God in all respects except that he was not Father. He had a distinctive

role. Son is not Father, but he was of the same power
to be.

Question: What is the relation between the human
and the divine in Christ?

Answer: The Chalcedonian Statement. A simple
answer would be that both humanity and divinity
must be held with equal tenacity and that they are
related to one another in Christ in a unique way
which can be described by using the concepts *nature*
and *person*. But the whole statement must be placed
before us.

> In agreement, therefore, with the holy fathers, we all
> unanimously teach that we should confess that our Lord
> Jesus Christ is one and the same Son, the same perfect
> in Godhead and the same perfect in manhood, truly God
> and truly man, the same of a rational soul and body,
> consubstantial with the Father in Godhead, and the same
> consubstantial with us in manhood, like us in all things
> except sin; begotten from the Father before the ages as
> regards His Godhead, and in the last days, the same,
> because of us and because of our salvation begotten from
> the Virgin Mary, the *Theotokos,* as regards His man-
> hood; one and the same Christ, Son, Lord, only-begotten,
> made known in two natures without confusion, without
> change, without division, without separation, the differ-
> ence of the natures being by no means removed because
> of the union, but the property of each nature preserved
> and coalescing in one *prosopon* and one *hypostasis*—not
> parted or divided into two *prosopa,* but one and the same
> Son, only-begotten, divine Word, the Lord Jesus Christ,
> as the prophets of old and Jesus Christ himself have

taught us about Him and the creed of our fathers has handed down.

(J. N. D. Kelly, *Early Christian Doctrines* [London: A. and C. Black, and New York: Harper, 1958], pp. 339-40).

First, note that Chalcedon picks up the two answers to the questions of humanity and divinity given before and puts them together in parallel:

> consubstantial with the Father in Godhead
> consubstantial with us in manhood, like us in all
>   things except sin

Second, note the use of the word *Theotokos,* which means God-bearing. Some had objected to this, by saying that Mary did not give birth to God. That was agreed but the Council wanted the word to mean that Jesus was divine from conception, thereby eliminating any last vestige of adoptionism.

Third, note how the words *nature, prosopon* (person literally "face"), *prosopa* (persons), and *hypostasis* (person) are used. To understand this critical aspect, let us summarize the significance of the whole statement. What did Chalcedon intend to say?

1. The true incarnation of the *logos* is the second person of the Godhead. By this is meant the actual assumption of the whole human nature into an everlasting union with the personality of the eternal *logos,* so that they constitute, from the moment of the conception, one undivided life forever. The incarnation,

the enfleshment of the Word, is neither a conversion
or transmutation of God into man, nor a conversion
of man into God. It is neither a mere indwelling of
God in man, nor an outward transitory connection of
the two.

2. Chalcedon made a distinction between nature and
person. *Nature* here means the same as *substance* in
the Nicene Creed. It is the name for the totality of
powers and qualities which constitute a being, that is,
its power to be what it is. This is not an extra energy
or a thing in itself but a language by which whatever
it is that gives existence to anything can be summarized in one word. It is not a matter or weight and
space idea at all. In fact, it has nothing to do with
space or with what can be seen or measured. It is a
concept, not a thing. It is a philosophical term which
interprets the meaning of an existence. This concept
was distinguished from *person* (which had two Greek
words, *prosopon* and *hypostasis,* because no one word
seemed to be adequate) by which they meant the acting subject of the substance. A person means the subject of the ego, the self-conscious, self-asserting, acting
center. It was assumed, rightly or wrongly, that two
dimensions to any living reality (God or man) could
be communicated by the use of two separate concepts
—person and nature. Whether they were wise or pro-
vincial in assuming this, their intention seems clear.

The concept of person here is not synonymous with the modern term *individual*. It is a bit closer to the word *personality* although this doesn't quite do it either.

3. The logos assumed not a human person (or we would have had two persons—a divine and a human) but a human nature which is common to all of us. It is not altogether clear whether Chalcedon meant the nature of *man* or *a* man. The matter may seem academic but it has some important repercussions later. This raises the question, did Christ achieve his personhood by virtue of the incarnation or was he a person separate from his relation to the *logos?* Some have solved this by saying that true manhood has a personality only in relationship with God. A man not related to God is therefore something less than a person in this sense of the word. If one insists that Christ had a human personality, it seems to me that he is using the word *person* in a different way than Chalcedon. Chalcedon had no intention of denying to Christ anything essential to human nature.

4. The result of the incarnation is the God-man. Christ is not a double being, with two persons, not a compound middle being, partly human and partly divine; but he is one person with two natures, one wholly human and one wholly divine.

5. Chalcedon emphasized the duality of the nature, but kept the human and the divine natures distinct. One is not to be confused with the other nor is one changed into the other. At the same time they are neither separable or divisible. The two natures interpenetrate each other and form one common life, one unity, yet forever remain human and divine. The two natures are entirely complete and embrace everything which pertains to each of them separately. Christ has all the powers of the Father in his divinity except that of being the Father and he has all the properties of Adam before the fall. Whether or not this means that he has two self-determinate centers of operation is a most difficult question not clearly answered by Chalcedon.

6. The unity of the person is another Chalcedonian affirmation. This is called the hypostatic union or the personal union. The union of the divine and human natures of Christ is a permanent state resulting from the incarnation, and it is a real, supernatural, personal, and inseparable union in distinction from any idea of absorption or confusion, or a moral union or a mystical union such as the oneness between the believer and Christ. The two natures constitute one personal life. Because of this union, whatever is said about the human nature can also be said of the divine and vice versa. One cannot divide the life of Christ into divine

and human acts (miracles are divine and anger is human, for example) except as a manner of speaking.

7. The whole work of Christ, therefore, is to be attributed to his person and not to the one or the other nature exclusively. The person is the acting subject, not the nature. Christ redeemed, not only in the sense that he was divine and his work was then infinite, or in the sense that he was human and his work was therefore meritorious, but primarily because these two possibilities were united into one person. This would have enormous implications for the interpretation of the work of Christ.

It is clear from this discussion that Chalcedon said "a plague on both your houses" to the extremes of Ebionitism and Docetism. No one starting point is adequate. Both are needed simultaneously. One is not more pious if he begins with the divine nor is he more impious if he begins with the human, but he is on dangerous ground in either case. The relation of the human and the divine is a paradox, firm, unbreakable. The incarnation is impossible if it hadn't happened.

The Durability of Chalcedon

Although from our rather unphilosophical and empirical prejudice this statement may seem terribly complicated, my opinion is that it has a remarkable resilience and applicability for us. Its purpose is not to wed the faith to a particular world view. Let us look at some of its strengths and weaknesses.

These are some of its strengths:

Limits are set to the range of speculation in Christology. A distorted Ebionitism or Docetism is not acceptable. At the same time it leaves a broad center for further interpretation.

A sufficient salvation is made possible for us. God is fully involved and man is fully involved.

Although it does not use biblical language, it pulls together the whole biblical witness in its variety. It does not eliminate any facet of the New Testament interest although at the same time it does not speak to every facet of Christology.

The mystery of God is preserved. Chalcedon does not add to the knowledge about God nor is it built on an unchallengeable doctrine of man. In this sense, it is a modest statement which is self-limiting.

Further development in Christology is permitted. Other questions than the ones specifically raised are not cut off. It does, however, commit all future discussion to the paradoxical relationship between humanity and divinity.

Weaknesses of Chalcedon are these:

Does Chalcedon have a secret and subtle tipping of the hat to Docetism? Is the one person-two nature formula with the one person being identified as the *logos* a concession to the domination of the divine?

To be sure, it does not intend this but is it subject to easy misinterpretation?

Chalcedon seems to make no distinction between the pre-resurrection or humiliated Christ and the post-resurrection or exalted Christ. In this significant? Some would say the radicality of the resurrection is not taken into account sufficiently. The Reformation would take up this question in more detail because of its importance for the doctrine of the real presence.

The emphasis is on the relation of the nature to the person rather than on the relation of the natures to each other in some direct way. Is this a weakness? The Lutheran tradition said yes and developed further a doctrine on how the divine nature "communicates" its powers to the human nature without changing the human nature.

Is the growth of the Jesus of Nazareth, clearly evident in Scripture, possible under this statement? Later discussion would take this up in detail and talk a great deal (without coming to a firm conclusion) about the so-called self-emptying of the God-man of his divine powers during his earthly life.

Are the categories of *person* and *nature* too impersonal, too static, too abstract to permit the kind of personal relationship to the Christ demanded by Scripture? Although Luther affirmed Chalcedonian Christology, he seemed to prefer St. Paul's approach more than St. John's and talked more easily of a dynamic relationship between God and man in Christ following St. Paul's phrase, "God was in Christ reconciling the world to himself."

Chalcedon and the Twentieth Century

Our task is not to discuss the developments since Chalcedon. We have characterized them as further interpretations, perhaps even additions, but not denials. If we confine ourselves to Chalcedon itself, we can see what enormous influence it ought to have for developing principles of interpretation of the whole faith. For example:

1. The divine and the human are never separated in God's work for us. God never appears pure or naked. "No one has seen God at any time." We "see" God in human form only. God's way of revealing himself to us is through the human. We ignore the human to our peril. We cannot sift God out from the human form in which he comes.

2. God does not reveal his grace to us in every human act. He reveals himself in particular acts of his choosing: the history of Israel, Christ himself, the New Testament interpretation of Christ, the communication of his word in human language and in acts called sacraments. This does not deny that God is hidden in every worldly act of both judgment and mercy.

3. God does not change the human into something divine in his work. Human remains human. Divine remains divine. Implications are that the Bible does not become less human because God speaks to us through it. The church does not become perfect or errorless because there God dwells and feeds his people. The bread does not turn into something supernatural because God's presence is mediated through it. We don't become divine because God dwells in us. Nature *bears* grace. It does not *become* grace. Nature retains its integrity. God retains his. Let God be God!

4. Man achieves a dignity undreamed of without the incarnation; God became man and bound himself to man forever. This is a gospel, a hope, an affirmation of love without parallel.

5. The intentions of Chalcedon can be expressed using other categories, other examples, other views of reality. In our day a series of proposals to interpret Chalcedon in language suitable to our day is one of the interesting products of theological speculation. We should not be so blind to the contributions of Chalcedon that we misinterpret its flexibility and its demands that we witness to our time the same salvation by the same God-man in ways as vigorous and far reaching and successful as they did.

4

The Question
of Communicating
the Christ Today

How does one communicate Jesus Christ in a secular age? How does one explain "who he is" in a time when men struggle with any concept of God and any real commitment to truth? I have said that the classical tradition of the Nicene and Chalcedonian creeds is still the faith of the church and I tried to show that the formulation of these creeds arose out of a concern for the mission of the church of that time. For the Christian well versed in the understanding of the Scriptures, these creeds still speak powerfully and adequately. I did not say that they were the *only* way to communicate the Christ. Let us explore the matter further.

Two attempts to proclaim the faith in our time I find inadequate for the task. The first is called "reductionism" and is represented by the view very vividly portrayed in Paul Van Buren's book *The Secular Meaning of the Gospel*. In an honest and thorough way, Professor Van Buren attempts to recast the faith in Jesus Christ in psychological categories, hoping thereby to find a way by which modern secular man can understand the Christian claim.

Jesus is described as an incandescent self who infects us with freedom. Van Buren maintains that the faith is not "taught" but "caught." The relationships among men are such that a mysterious kind of communication can occur which causes one man to be profoundly affected by the communication which occurs by the very existence of others. The idea itself perhaps cannot be denied. In fact, it is a most intriguing kind of suggestion.

The difficulty is that Van Buren applies this idea in such a way that it minimizes the historical content of the Scriptures and any real possibility of describing in understandable terms the relation of God and man in Jesus. He "reduces" the faith to this kind of "effect" that Jesus has on me. I would say that this reduces the faith beyond the limits required by the classical Christology as necessary to the continuance of the Christian tradition. It may be, on occasion, an effective preaching tool, but it is not an adequate theology.

The second attempt I would call "mathematical theology." This view assumes that there is one perfect systematic theology which is fully adequate for the task of communication and is the theology which is to be learned and taught. It is something like Euclid's geometry which is built on certain unchallengeable axioms from which a whole system of truth is logically deduced. This system is so closely argued and interwoven that no one part of it may be challenged or the whole house will fall. There can be only one answer to every question and every legitimate question has an answer. This encapsules the Christian into one philosophy of truth and one understanding of how truth is known and communicated. Basic presuppositions are thus defined "prior" to the faith. The philosophical foundations become irreducible propositions for the faith itself. For example, the inerrancy of Scripture as interpreted in the context of this approach would mean that "I believe in the inerrancy of the Scripture" is a necessary faith commitment prior to saying "I believe that Jesus Christ is my Lord."

As a philosophical possibility, this kind of theology has a certain attraction. It means that there are no "open" questions, no ambiguities, and there can be no real areas of dispute. If reasonable men can be brought to see the logic of the basic assumptions, the acceptance of the whole faith would naturally follow.

The chief difficulty with this theology is that this is not the way the Scripture itself communicates the faith. The Bible is not a completely integrated logical system requiring believing because of the perfection of the system, but rather a revelation of God's grace which engenders a response of faith. It utilizes a host of witnesses and many kinds of communication in order to provide the means for the Spirit to evoke man's trust.

If these two extremes are not the whole answer, what is? Fortunately the Bible is a never-ending source of rich suggestions for preaching the gospel in any age. But our first task is to look at the characteristics of our age to see what problems we face.

Factors to Be Considered

Four especially significant factors must be considered before we attempt to outline ways of communicating.

1. The Character of the New Testament Witness

We suggested above that the Bible is not a completely integrated logical system which compels belief by virtue of that character. It rather is a powerful witness to the event of God's revelation in Jesus Christ, telling us of that event and interpreting it for us in a variety of ways in order that we may see its profundity and simplicity. It is a "means of grace," that is, the way by which the Spirit evokes faith by judging us, preaching to us, comforting us, teaching us, prodding us. In doing so, the Bible uses a tremendous variety of communicative tools. There is not one formula which is merely repeated over and over, but an almost never-ending series of confessions of faith set in different contexts, said by different kinds of people, purposefully directed into different situations and capturing a myriad of moods.

All of these communication efforts are directed towards one end—the response of faith. They center on one object—Jesus Christ. They have one organizing principle—salvation by grace. The audience towards which they ultimately aim is one—all of mankind— and that means also the varying cultural situations in all history which include the secular man of today.

What we need to do is to discover and utilize the richness of this witness for our communication.

2. The New Sense of History

There was a time when history was understood in a rather simplistic way—as past events communicated to us by the use of language which recreates that history for us in the present so that we can rationally grasp and understand it. This works in most instances. The factual element in history can be communicated and can be accepted if the listener is convinced that the evidence supporting the communication is reasonable.

But what about that kind of reporting that seeks

to communicate the "significance" of an event? That Jesus was born of the Virgin Mary is the kind of event that can be accepted or rejected, but what is its *meaning*? What is the evidence for such an event? Can it be historically proved or verified in any way? Or must we use the word "history" in a different sense in speaking about the virgin birth?

Being born of a virgin, as an event in itself without any concern for meaning, is only an interesting scientific oddity. To give meaning to that event, an interpretation must be added by someone who speaks at a later time. The reception of that interpretation in the present becomes another kind of history—not the history of provable facts but the history of ideas, the history of what men in the past have believed.

We are beginning to see that history is a more profound phenomenon than pure fact. If, as we Christians believe, history has a purpose, and Jesus Christ is God's purpose for all men and all history, then that interpretative meaning of the Christ must be communicated and not just the accounts of his life. In fact, that "extra" element becomes the important matter.

Historical reporting has a *new* sense, for we have opened up the possibility of more than one interpretation. In the case of a profound event, several interpretations are necessary to fully realize all its implications. The resurrection of Jesus, for example, has a more profound meaning than simply the coming to life of a dead man. A full understanding of this event requires a whole series of interpretations in order that we might get even a small glimpse into all that God has in mind for his world. Indeed, it might even require a New Testament of twenty-seven books!

3. The Nature of Language

One of the fascinating developments in our century has been the investigation into the nature of language. We have learned that language is not a simple entity. There are different kinds of language. There is a kind of language which is used to convey information. Every word in that kind of language mirrors a fact in the world and can be investigated to see if it is true. But there is also a kind of language that seeks to cause a response in people, such as fear, joy, trust, or anger. This kind of language has a power *in itself*. One does not investigate the world to which this language refers to discover its meaning but rather the results engendered in the person who hears it.

It follows that different kinds of language have different kinds of logic, different rules for their behavior. Poetry is not the same as historical reporting, a parable not the same as a philosophical essay, a confession of faith not the same as a judgment, a declaration of love not the same as an argument.

It also follows that language adapts itself to the nature of the thing communicated. An event is not the same kind of reality as a tree, a person is not communicated the same way as an idea, a mood is talked about differently than a law, a promise has characteristics that give it an aura strikingly its own which is to be differentiated from the language of condemnation. And how does one talk about a miracle? Or God?

The marvel is that the Bible was a great language textbook before language analysis came into being in the twentieth century. We must learn from the Bible rather than make quick assumptions that language is something we understand innately or completely.

4. The Death of Substantialist Philosophy

That may be a strong statement. The question is, can modern man understand the Christian faith communicated with the presuppositions of reality into which the classic Christian confession was cast? I have already said that the Christian—although he uses modern presuppositions of reality—can understand these classic confessions and apply their message to today. But can modern secular man do likewise? Modern man lives in a world of protons, electrons, energy, matter, not in a world which understands or accepts the language of substance, divinity, universal, ideas, spirit, and being. Can he find the statements of faith in this latter world and put them to use in his life today? That is his challenge. The church must help him.

One can perhaps argue the point, but I believe that we can no longer assume that talking about Jesus Christ in only one way—the language of the Nicene Creed—either communicates as it once did or does justice to all of the communication tools the Bible gives us. You must answer this question for yourself. Is talk about the meaning of being the most helpful way to communicate your faith in Jesus Christ?

The Method of Models

Our purpose is to communicate the most important event in history in order to evoke a response of trust. That event is a person we believe to be both God and man. Our task is not easy but we have help!

Ian Ramsey in his book *Models and Mystery* (London: Oxford University Press, 1964) suggests that we utilize the biblical method of developing models. A model is a collection of distinctive, reliable, and specific techniques for talking about a reality which is ultimately mysterious. We must seek to create in the listener's mind a picture, an insight, a concept which is more than and different from the language of words. Just as a scientist builds a model or an architect makes a three-dimensional replica of what he is proposing to build, so the preacher must find ways to communicate a sense of the Christ which is more than a collection of words. This is what the New Testament does in a rather simple way with its many descriptive terms for Jesus: king, light, bread, shepherd, son, judge, door, and many more. The Old Testament in its original Hebrew works with pictures, with models, more than with the logic of a string of sentences.

A model must have four basic characteristics:

1. A model is necessary when that which is to be communicated is not itself available for display. One would not build a model of a tree when trees are available but one might attempt to model an atom. The reality itself cannot be seen, but it is nevertheless a reality to the communicator. The communicator knows that which he wishes to communicate, but ordinary language and ordinary description fall short of the task. The reality to be communicated thus participates in mystery.

2. The model must make use of a universal human experience so that the listener, who does not know the reality to be communicated, nevertheless recog-

nizes a reality in his own life which gives him a "connection." This primary recognition begins communication. The assumption is that there is in everyday human life sufficient experience with mystery and with various categories of communication to enable contact to be made. The listener does not by virtue of this recognition believe, but he is able to hear, and is confronted with the possibility of believing.

3. The communicator accepts the condition that the model is not in and of itself the reality communicated. No language or picture of Jesus Christ is Jesus Christ himself. No model is divine, perfect, or the object of faith. The model is meant to point beyond itself, not to become an idol in itself. Building models is like drawing a rectangle in a circle. Take a sheet of paper, draw a large circle, and then draw as many rectangles in that circle as you can. You will notice several interesting results.

- You can draw many rectangles of different sizes —in fact, an infinite number.

- No rectangle completely encompasses the full area of the circle—there is always some of the circle "left over."

- Every rectangle has within its own area the center of the circle. You cannot draw a rectangle which does not include the center.

This suggests that no proper model can miss the point and thus fail to help communicate, but no one model does the full job or ever displaces or equals that which is communicated.

4. The purpose of the model is to communicate. It is not intended to draw attention to itself but to provide the means for the Spirit to draw a response from the listener to the reality communicated. The model, therefore, eventually drops away having accomplished its task.

This theory of communication is not so different from what the church has always tried to do. This has been strikingly true in the interpretation of the atonement. The church has never incorporated the whole teaching of the atonement in the New Testament into any creed, but through the centuries it has preached, taught, and believed in several models, pictures, or theories of the atonement. I have described these in the book *His Only Son Our Lord,* but I suspect that they are well-known to most Christians.

The preceding discussion of models has prepared us to think about models in speaking about Christ. I find four models helpful in communicating insights to answer the question, "How are God and Man related in Jesus Christ?" These models are the four universal human experiences: being, act, sight, and hearing.

The Model of Being

The classical Christology described in the preceding chapter is really an exercise in model building with "being" as its model. Using the Johannine verse, "The Word became flesh and dwelt among us," our early fathers assumed that an intuition of being was a universal human experience. They sought to build a bridge of communication between the biblical language of Word and flesh to a concept of "being" widely accepted in the culture of that time. They were, as we have said, remarkably successful, and their model was adopted as a universal Christian creed.

Because we described this so fully, we shall not repeat the reasoning except to remind ourselves of the basic picture—there is in Jesus Christ a *duality of natures in one person.*

The question here is whether or not we can assume that a concept of being, as they understood it, is a universal human experience for this generation. Some say so. The school of existentialism we described in the first chapter would say so. There is given to every human existence the power of disclosedness, a self-understanding which appears to every person who reflects on his existence.

Theologians who find this approach to reality to coincide with their own experience consider this model to be very much alive for our time. Paul Tillich was perhaps the leading exponent of this view. Professor John Macquarrie, a disciple of Tillich, has developed this theory in his book *Principles of Christian Theology* (New York: Scribner's, 1966). Whether or not one agrees, or even understands the intricate philosophical reasoning of men such as these, the truth of the formula *two natures in one person* cannot be denied by any Christian.

Our purpose, however, is to discover other biblical insights to deal with the same goal of communicating who Jesus is.

The Model of Act

Let us turn to Paul. In 2 Corinthians 5:19, Paul says, "God was in Christ reconciling the world to himself." God was *in* Christ. God was reconciling. Paul characteristically uses verbs rather than nouns to communicate the relation of God and man in Jesus. God was acting through Jesus in accomplishing his salvation for men, a salvation he calls reconciliation. Is there any way we can construct a model related to our own experience which might illumine for us how God could be in a man?

How does a person act? What kind of an event is a person? Aside from the question of his nature or substance, how does a person live in himself? The Bible has many words to describe what a person is

—words such as body, soul, heart, spirit. The Bible teaches that each person is a unity, but a unity with many complex forces at work. A person can be viewed from a number of perspectives—the way he appears in the world of space and time (body), the way he appears from the perspective of his inner life (soul), the way he appears as he expresses himself, his personality (spirit), or the way he acts in exercising his powers of decision making through his will (heart).

These various activities of a person sometimes are in conflict with each other. Paul spoke of the phenomenon in the wonderfully graphic passage in Romans 7:15-20:

> I do not understand my own actions. For I do not do what I want, but I do the very thing I hate. Now if I do what I do not want, I agree that the law is good. So then it is no longer I that do it, but sin which dwells within me. For I know that nothing good dwells within me, that is, in my flesh. I can will what is right, but I cannot do it. For I do not do the good I want, but the evil I do not want is what I do. Now if I do what I do not want, it is no longer I that do it, but sin which dwells within me.

This is an intensely paradoxical way of viewing the variety of forces at work within each person. It is I, says Paul, and yet it is not I. Can we put it in another way? Augustine spoke of the experience of these various "I's" as a conversation within us. We can scold

ourselves, lecture ourselves, argue with ourselves, re-
joice together, so to speak, in ourselves. It is as though
there were several "selves" in us. There appears to be
in us an "acting self," an inner self which is the point
from which we "see" ourselves and the world. This
inner self "speaks" to and is related to a transcendent
self, which stands over against the inner self. These
two selves, sometimes called flesh and spirit in Paul,
are in conflict in all of us. Every man experiences
the anxiety of this conflict and falls into sin against
his own will because there is no harmony, no reconciliation between these selves.

Could we use this experience to suggest that God
was at work in Christ as a transcendent self, con-
trolling, instructing, leading Jesus as well as permit-
ting the inner self to relate freely and wholly to the
transcendent self? The anxiety and sin which is the
lot of every ordinary human being was then completely overcome in Jesus of Nazareth. God was fully
operative in him and Jesus was fully dependent on
him. He was at the same time a full human being
and yet God was fully at work in him. In complete
harmony with God, and so completely reconciled to
God, he became the reconciliation with which God
reconciled himself to the world and the world to
himself.

This would mean that Jesus participated fully in
the human experience and yet in such a way that he

was sinless. Or as Paul says in Colossians 1:19, "For in him all the fulness of God was pleased to dwell, and through him to reconcile to himself all things, whether on earth or in heaven, making peace by the blood of his cross."

The model we use as a bridge is our experience of our own sin, the conflicts I believe every person experiences in himself.

In a time when the anxiety levels of men are high —and no matter what his view of the world every man experiences tensions and conflicts in himself—is it possible to communicate a person who overcomes each possible temptation and conflict by a complete inner reconciliation and thus becomes the example for all men, indeed their Savior?

God was in Christ reconciling. Who could not be intrigued by such a possibility and deeply desirous of sharing such a marvelous gift?

The Model of Sight

Let us return to John. In the very same verse in which he tells us that the Word became flesh and dwelt among us, John goes on to say, "We have beheld his glory, glory as of the only Son from the Father." (John 1:14) Two models in one sentence!

John is saying that when we see Jesus we see God. He is suggesting that there are two kinds of sight:

the empirical seeing that all men share, for Jesus of Nazareth is in full view in history so that all men can see if they care to look; and a "faith" seeing which some men see and all could see. When God heals our blindness we see in Jesus a glory which is hidden from us when we see him only as a historical figure. There is an inner insight, a gift of understanding, which sees more than that which is revealed in the ordinary looking on.

Every man experiences this two-fold kind of seeing. There is the kind of seeing that we all share in observing other persons. If we have the gift of physical sight we have no difficulty in seeing other persons about us. But when we get to "know" some persons intimately we begin to see more than that which we observe through our eyes. We "see" their personality, their true selves, and we develop a knowledge of them which is different from the empirical knowledge of weight and height and physical features. We develop a relationship with these persons which is very special, and a mysterious phenomenon called love occurs. This phenomenon is of several kinds—love for parents, love for brothers and sisters, and erotic love for the opposite sex. In current language there is also a "soul" love.

Jesus can be called God's symbol—that is, he shares in the reality of what God is because he becomes the revelation of God's love. He identifies God. What he is becomes for us what God is because Jesus and God become the same "appearance" for us. We might say that there is a duality of vision but one revelation, one person seen.

Love is such a powerful force in the human experience that men should recognize the possibility that Jesus can evoke the power of love in such a way as to reveal God himself.

The Model of Hearing

Let us try another. Jesus said, "He who has ears to hear, let him hear." In fact, he said it over and over: Matthew 11:15, 13:9, 13:16, 13:43; Mark 4:9, 4:23, 7:16, 8:18; Luke 8:8, 14:35. The Book of Revelation picks up the idea "He who has an ear, let him hear what the Spirit says to the churches." Revelation 2:7, 11, 17, 29; 3:6, 13, 22; 13:9. And there are others.

The Bible further pictures God as "speaking." "And God said" is a constant refrain. Hebrews puts it succinctly: "In many and various ways God spoke of old to our fathers by the prophets; but in these last days he has spoken to us by a Son." Hebrews 1:1. Luther and the Reformation put great emphasis on the "speaking God" and out of this comes the fundamental theological category of the "Word of God." The Lutheran tradition accordingly has put great stress on the beautiful words of Paul:

But how are men to call upon him in whom they have
not believed? And how are they to believe in him of
whom they have never heard? And how are they to
hear without a preacher? And how can men preach
unless they are sent? As it is written, "How beautiful
are the feet of those who preach good news!" But they
have not all heeded the gospel; for Isaiah says, "Lord,
who has believed what he has heard from us?" So faith
comes from what is heard, and what is heard comes by
the preaching of Christ. (Romans 10:14-17)

"So faith comes from what is heard," clearly "hearing" is a biblical model. God speaks. We listen. Faith
comes.

The phenomenon of hearing is a unity, that is,
when we speak or listen to others speaking we use
words without thinking about the difference between
the sounds we hear and the thoughts they communicate. Hearing refers both to the physical sounds which
occur and to the meaning of those sounds. It is a
single experience.

However, when we reflect about what has happened,
we can become conscious of the difference between the
words and the thoughts which they transmit. We
can distinguish theoretically between two levels:
spoken language and received meaning. We know
that the same idea can be conveyed by different sets
of sounds, different words, even different languages.
At the level of event, we have unity. At the level of
analysis and reflection we have a duality. It is possible
to hear words without receiving the meaning, or re-

ceiving a different meaning. We must have "ears to hear" what is meant to be said—what the "Spirit is saying."

Jesus is God's Word to us. Those who hear in faith hear not only what he says in words, hear not only what he is as Jesus of Nazareth, a man of Palestine, but hear what he means, that is, what God is saying through him. The hearing of faith hears a revelation of God and not just the words of a man.

We see the same pattern emerging—a unity in duality. Those who wish to hear all that is said must hear at two levels through one thing said.

I believe that hearing as unity and duality is a universal human experience. We all know what difficulty we humans have in achieving full communication. We have experienced over and over again the phenomenon of hearing someone speak but not understanding him. We have to listen again—and again —we have to have ears to hear.

Every secular man should be willing to admit the possibility that he has not properly heard Jesus *the Word*. And we should be able to establish the first step in serious dialog by suggesting that in Jesus Christ we have a dual dimension of hearing that requires the kind of involvement that penetrates the words to "hear" what he claimed. It is our faith as Christians that these words themselves have power and authority to communicate God in such a way as to elicit a response of trust which does not depend on a philosophy of reality as a prior understanding or commitment. God can be communicated directly through his Word, God comes alive to the listener in the hearing of the Word, the Word who is called Jesus.

A Quick Summary

There are other models, of course. Another chapter or book would be necessary to deal with them all. These we have mentioned are true to the task we have accepted.

- All contribute to the focal question—how is Jesus both God and man—both a historical phenomenon and a message from God?

- None of them attempts to solve the mystery. They neither explain it nor take its place. They attempt only to communicate, to cause men to respond.

- They are all true to the New Testament, indeed are models in the New Testament itself.

- None of them requires any prior commitment to any particular philosophy, any particular understanding of history or nature or man. But they utilize experience which men already acknowledge without challenge.

- All of them preserve the fundamental and classical Christological formula—Jesus Christ is both a duality and a unity. He is one and at the same time full and true man and full and true God.

Yes, Jesus Christ can be communicated today. The secular age is not an impossible age in which to proclaim Christ. It is only an interesting challenge.

5

The Question
of the Church

The age in which we live, and that means, the way we are in this age, precludes our grasping reality as a "thing," an object. We are not sure we can answer the question, "What is the being of anything?" This becomes insuperably difficult when we ask, "What is the being of the church?" That substance, that power, that reality of the church is mystery. The church is something God has done, someone he has chosen, a faith he has engendered and a hope he has given. It shares in the mystery of God's own being and acts. We can no more explain the being of the church than we can explain *being itself*. But we can *say* a great deal about the church. By examining the church's source, function, and manifestations in the world and our own involvement and encounter with the church, we can create a language that has meaning and communicates, in the symbol and logic of language, the reality which we designate church. The church is a phenomenon to be spoken of, reflected about and analyzed, but it is primarily a reality to be confessed.

The New Testament and the Church

When I examine the New Testament documents, I find that the church is a principal category. It is not one item among many nor is it historically secondary; that is, it does not come about because of what men do after some preceding event such as faith. The church is woven into the whole texture of New Testament thought. The dozens of symbols testify to this. It is not a question of the individual's finding a relationship to God and then deciding to form a community. Rather God creates a people, works with a people, redeems a people, and men are called to be people and discover their personhood. One cannot discuss the faith without an ecclesiology.

But I do not discover a systematic ecclesiology in the New Testament. There is rather a variety of traditions. The church is seen from many perspectives.

No single starting point governs a subsequent formulation of the mystery. One cannot take the preaching of the kingdom, or the baptism of Jesus, or the confession of Peter, or the words of Jesus to Peter, or the cross, or the resurrection, or the outpour-

ing of the Spirit as a single determinative and de-
cisive source event. All Christian traditions have been
somewhat guilty of doing this. Rather, all beginning
points belong to the question of the church. All contribute. Each corrects, reminds, adds to, and each
denies any final grasp of the mystery. The whole
Christ event itself is the source.

Nor is there any clear historical principle which
suggests that the New Testament works through a
process bringing final clarity out of chaos, presenting
to us in a late epistle the final and full judgment of
the Christian community as to what it is. The whole
New Testament is a witness. The variety belongs to
the fullness. There is no culminating final word.

What I do find is a strong sense of continuity. The
New Testament pictures a new manifestation of
God's redemptive power but not a new God or an
altogether new people. Jesus did not begin the church.
He rather began a new age of the church which has
both a continuity and a discontinuity with the redemptive deeds of God that went before.

I also find a strong sense of history. The church is
understood to be deeply embedded in the processes
of time. It has a past and a future. It partakes of the
age in which it lives. The church of the New Testament is itself historically conditioned with particular
problems and needs. The wrenching away from the
synagogue, the Middle East culture, the cosmological

commitments, the mission oriented function, and other influences determined its particular character. It would be impossible to duplicate its life in the world of another age, but it would be equally impossible for us to cut ourselves off from the apostolic church, for not only is that church the authoritative witness to the revelation, but it is *our own* memory and therefore *our own* history.

The church in the New Testament is always understood as a confessing community. The community believes and therefore becomes what it is by being involved in what it is. The church is none other than the life of faith.

And I find the word *freedom* extraordinarily suggestive of the church's life. The church is bound, but in this slavery has become free to act and to live in its own time. It is possible for the church to speculate concerning the faith, to make explicit what is implicit, to consider the inferences of the revelation, but the church is always bound to what is *really* given and within that givenness finds freedom.

Two New Testament words bring these ideas together. The first is *ekklesia* from which by a torturous route we get our English word *church*. The church is the called-out people, a community. This should always be accompanied by the possessive, "of God." The church is a people of God. Any designation of its reality must say this. No other category of being can displace this. This people is a God-created people. God is the initiator, the one who calls. The church has no being in itself, no authority, no life apart from God.

The second is the great phrase *soma tou Christou,* the body of Christ. This phrase admits of many interpretations, but it surely means without question that the church belongs to Jesus Christ. We have here the great integrating idea in the diversity. The body of Christ expresses both the intimacy of the union of the church with Christ and the distinction of the church *from* Christ. Christ is its life. He works in the church. In him, the church coheres and has her being. The church is subject to him in every way, participates in him, loves him, obeys him, and thus finds and exercises the freedom he bestows. This also means an intimate unity of the members that binds them together, gives them an integrity and essential role in being themselves as well as being his. Life in the church is the same as life taken up in Christ which involves personal encounter and participation in the hope of the fulfillment that is to come.

We can also use the language of Spirit. This life in him is a new quality of existence we call the presence of his spirit. This *koinonia* has gifts and fruits and these gifts and fruits conform to the shape of Christ's life. His role as servant, his dependence on God, his love for the unlovely, his openness to neighbor, his complete involvement in this world, his forgiving attitude, his conflict with evil, his prayer life and other descriptive phrases can be used to characterize the church in its daily obedience and responsibilities.

The sociological dimension of the church is thus assumed in the New Testament picture of the church. It is a visible people with a hidden life. In its concreteness the church exhibits the brokenness of all human life, shares in the sins and trauma of all mankind, is affected by and reacts to the same forces that afflict all men. It thus has the capacity for growth and decay, repentance and renewal, unfaithfulness and faithfulness. But the church also worships, develops its forms of discipline and service, and to the surprise of no one, reflects on its faith and produces a theology. The cultus and the structure of the church are categories which are both possible and necessary to discuss.

The Signs of the Church in the World

How is this church known to us now? How does it manifest itself among us? To communicate this understanding, we in our tradition have developed a rather complex language based on the phrase, "Word of God."

Man finds himself in the world without his own request and without an understanding of why. He discovers that the world is full of conflict, even hostility. Death threatens him. He seems unable to cope with a myriad of daily problems and time goes inexorably on. His existence is given and seemingly with this a hunger for meaning. But the world seems silent in return to his entreaties for answers. He seems unable to help himself except in the limited area of self-preservation.

Into this silent world God comes in actions and words, first in the history of Israel and then in the event of our Lord. God comes to man where man is and he always comes through the events that are part of his already given existence. Revelation is particularized in events and interpreted in language forming a tradition. The God of past events speaks to us in this age through the words of that past interpreted and through acts performed in our own midst. We mean, of course, the authoritative words of the Scripture, made alive through Christian testimony and preaching, acts of love of many dimensions, and particular definable acts we call sacraments.

These events and words are public, available for all men to see, and thus subject to analysis but powerful only in the encounter in which faith is created. These are all words of God, the reality of God made present —the prophetic history of Israel, Jesus Christ in his person, words, and deeds, the witness to him in the Scriptures, the words empowered by the Spirit in our own day, and the dramatic acts called sacraments. They each have their own particular form and purpose, but they each and all communicate the same gospel, the same life, and create the same church.

Because of the way we have defined sacrament in our tradition, only two, Baptism and the Eucharist, are called sacraments. Other acts, such as prayer and preaching, may also be understood to be gracious acts communicating God's mercy and power, but we have not used the word sacrament to describe them.

The point is that the same power which created the New Testament community creates the people of God today. The signs of the church are the same, summarized in the phrase *word and sacrament*. This people of God is in continuity with the church of the past, but lives in a new age, with the same problems and same redemption as the church of any past age. The quality of life, the freedom, and the destiny are the same.

Baptism is the effective sign of initiation into this body of Christ. The Eucharist is the effective sign of renewal in which the risen Lord is present under the signs of bread and wine, giving himself to his people to eat and to drink. In this celebration of grace the people of God identify themselves with the Christ, his sacrifice and his exaltation, and receive anew the saving grace of God the Father. The spoken word communicates the same renewing grace. The form of the communication, the time, and the language differ. The effect is the same. And the living Lord is present in each of these manifestations. The sign is different. It is the same Lord and the same presence.

The Reformation and the Church

The Reformation spoke of the church in its own way, conditioned by its own concerns and problems. It defined the church as the communion of saints, or people of God among whom the Word is preached and the sacraments are administered according to the gospel. This definition was a working principle, not a final and all inclusive dogma. It sought to approach the mystery of the church with a functional methodology. The people of God are created by God's work, work designated as the preached gospel and the sacraments. The grace of God is particularized, communicated, celebrated, believed, and lived in the context of these events. The church then can be seen to have an "event" character. The mystery of the people of God can be described in phenomenological or act language. This surely is not the only way to speak of the church, but it is a useful and faithful way.

The Reformation approach emphasizes three points:

First, it draws attention to the living character of the church. The church is a believing community, an acting community, a hoping community. The church is pointed to as a community which responds in faith. The boundaries of the church are not in themselves finally described. The gospel—in language and act— is emphasized, and faith as the response to that gospel, becomes a focus of attention.

Second, the Reformation seeks a certain simplicity in its language. The most profound commitment can sometimes be said simply. Its simplicity should not be interpreted as lacking sophistication or showing philosophical naievete. Philosophical commitments can then to a large degree be avoided while at the same time the gospel and spirit accomplish their work. The message of the Word of God is emphasized rather than its dogmatic definition. The role of the laymen in theological reflection becomes possible and entanglements with the subtleties of psychologizing minimized.

The Reformation, thirdly, worked with the principle of simultaneity. It is possible for us to say that the Word of God constitutes the church and in the same breath faith constitutes the church. It is possible to call the church holy and realize that this people of God sins. It is even necessary to speak of the responsibility of man and the free gift of grace. It is incumbent to realize that man does not take even one step toward God. God walks all the way to man, but man is completely involved in his whole being in the response of faith. Freedom can be emphasized under the authority of the gospel. The church is a continuity with the past but an ever renewing creation of the present. The church is being yet always becoming. The church is both the means to an end and the end itself.

The context of this language is a commitment to the emphases that we find in the church fathers. They defined four attributes of the church—unity, holiness, catholicity, and apostolicity. The church is one, for there is only one Lord, one creating gospel, one resultant people—as divided or as unfaithful as they may appear to be in the world. The church is holy, for one spirit works in it, forgiving, renewing, making holy in the eyes of God. The church is catholic, knowing no boundaries that limit its destiny. The church is apostolic, always tied to its source and memory, identifying the same Lord in its whole history and exhibiting the same faith, though language and emphases and context may vary with time and place and faithfulness.

The Reformation did not seek to separate itself from the church catholic. The confessions of the Lutheran tradition are basically irenic, seeking identification with the church universal in all past history. The many unfortunate events of the past four centuries which have made each of our traditions sometimes explicitly deny the unity of the church except in terms of its own life and often build high walls of separation, even in terms of recognition and love, should not be attributed as the true interpretation of our theological tradition. Part of our joy in a more ecumenical age is our ability to overcome some of these presumptuous attitudes. Nevertheless the Reformation churches consider themselves true and full churches, faithful to the people of God revealed in the New Testament, while admitting that they are historically conditioned in language, life, and even in understanding.

The Ministry

The ministry is of the essence of the church. If the gospel creates the church, if the sacraments are the necessary signs of God's presence and grace, then a ministry is necessary. "How shall they hear without a preacher?" Only a mystical ecclesiology could conceive of a people of God without a ministry.

The New Testament displays a variety of ministries as well as layers of tradition in ecclesiology. In our view, no one sole and exclusive ministry prevailed from the start or had been authorized by our Lord in advance or could be viewed as classical and normative. The primitive ministry was not presbyterian or episcopal or congregational or charismatic. The Christian community could in its freedom select the form or the combination of forms for its ministry in the post New Testament era but could not decide, in its own wisdom alone, that one type was normative.

In our tradition we have used the functional formula again. The minister is one who performs certain functions, preaches, teaches, counsels, administers the sacrament. He is called by the church, ordained by the laying on of hands, given the authority which belongs to the gospel, and assigned certain administrative responsibilities. He is priest, shepherd, preacher, teacher, and hopefully prophet. The validity of the ministry, if that is the best term to use, would mean for us a ministry authorized by the church and understood therefore as one called by God.

I would admit that this approach has a certain depersonalization. The Reformation tradition has been chary to speak of the person of the minister, preferring to think rather of the office of the ministry which the person fills. The reason for this is that our tradition has wanted to be careful not to suggest that the grace of God which redeems man is of a hierarchical order with a more powerful grace preserved for the ordained ministry. The minister, too, is a sinner saved by grace. But in actual thought and use, the person of the minister is described in terms of a certain *charisma*. The minister must be a person with a living faith, apt to teach and preach, educable in the understanding of the faith, dedicated to his task, the master of certain arts of ministering to people, disciplined in his life and called by God, that is, he must be a volunteer with a sense of vocation. There is a grace for the ministry that has its own form although it is the same grace God gives all men for their particular needs and vocations.

Ordination is the public attestation to this *charisma* and authority. It certainly has a sense of continuity and therefore succession, for the minister receives his office from those who went before him. He is committed to the apostolic witness, and he hands down to the generations that come after him the tradition of the faith. The difficulty among churches seems to lie in a disagreement as to what constitutes a normative authority for succession and not in the concept of succession itself.

We emphasize heavily the lay ministry, but distinguish between public and private ministry. Public ministry is that recognized ordained ministry authorized by the church. Although we recognize varieties of ministry, we have not distinguished orders in the ministry aside from the two, public and private. The priesthood of all believers means that every Christian is to minister to his brother, assist him in every need, hear his confession, and testify to the gospel. It does not mean that every man is authorized to administer the Lord's Supper, although in emergencies he may administer Baptism.

The church as organized today reflects too clearly past ages and societies. It seems to the outsider to be more like a feudal society or paternalistic family structure than a vital and free people of God. Whatever may be the final disposition regarding ways to articulate the meaning of the ministry, we believe that the Lord's Supper belongs to the Lord. He is the host and he has promised to be present wherever faithful people of God gather, remember his promises and share together his gifts of bread and wine.

6

The Question
of the Reformation
in the Modern Age

My purpose is to reflect on the thesis that Reformation theology is viable for the modern man. This is a way to get at such questions as: Can one be a Lutheran in the 1970s? What is the meaning of the Reformation claims in the light of the concerns and the mind-set of this generation? Does the Reformation heritage restrict or encourage open inquiry? These have once again become real questions in the Lutheran community in America. If the shape of understanding the Reformation gives us can be clarified, some of the other questions in this secular age with which we wrestle may be easier to handle. The mission of the church grows out of a right understanding of a reflection on the faith which we call theology.

First, we shall consider three introductory themes concerning the methodology of Reformation theology and then outline more fully five thrusts which I call faith commitments of the Reformation heritage.

The Reformation identified the source of authority for the faith with the slogan *sola scriptura*. It was based on the idea that both knowledge and authority have a single source. One must find and locate that single particular system for method or truth or authority and make that one commitment govern and regulate all else. This was a typical development in the Western mind and we are still caught by this temptation. We often think that we must choose between the scientific method and the inner life as sources for answers to ultimate questions. We can't tolerate both as sources of illumination. One of the struggles of our modern world is to accept pluralism, whether of authorities or epistemologies or races or ethical systems.

Sola scriptura is wrongly understood if it is used to suggest that the Scriptures are the *only* source of all knowledge or the final and regulating authority for *all* questions with which men must deal. The Scriptures are the sole authority *for the faith*. This faith commitment not only frees man, but requires him to be involved in other questions of authority and knowledge for his mission in the world.

A second note as an introduction is Luther's breathtaking reductionism. The Reformation was a process of reducing the faith to the essentials. It was made clear that the Christian conscience was bound only by God's clear word and command. This unleashed in Western history a movement of relentless and limitless criticism. In theology it resulted in the formal declaration of the death of God by those few who have followed this method ruthlessly to a final, logical conclusion.

At the same time, Western man has been engaged in an intensive examination of everything about him and even of himself. He cannot let the world be. He doesn't listen to the Beatles' song, "Let It Be." He must analyze and criticize and reduce until he has found that out of which everything is made. This has been a powerful drive in the Western world, a powerful force for good in the search for truth. But when unattached to some fundamental commitment, it is self-defeating, for it ultimately destroys everything. Man is too clever and too demonic to play God. In the process he destroys not only himself but his understanding of God as well.

A third example is the effect of Luther's so-called individualism, unhappily misunderstood often by both the Lutheran community and the society in which it lives. There is nevertheless no disputing that Luther's lone stand against his professors, then his superiors, and finally against both pope and emperor until such time as he, Luther, should be personally convinced, on the basis of Scripture and reason that he was wrong, gave invincible theological sanction to the notion of the sovereign conscience. This touched off the rampant sectarianism which resulted in many denominations, each mutually excluding the others. This strong addiction to the ability of every man to be right became the undergirding slogan for political and social movements which still reverberate among us.

For Luther, the situation was saved by the *sola scriptura* and by his concept of the church as the community of God. For him, strangely and perhaps to some, paradoxically, these went together, a single authority, a single conscience and a single people of God. But for the man without this faith commitment, the freedom of conscience to deny all has been both the source of heroic efforts of man to save himself and the source of demonic efforts to destroy all but himself. So we have in Reformation methodology some problems which still haunt us and which I believe have much to say about the way Christian communities operate.

I want to reflect on five faith commitments in an attempt to capture some of the underlying motifs of the Reformation stance which might be helpful in answering the question of the mission of the church.

The Humanity of Man

The Reformation was essentially a revolt against the Middle Ages at the beginning of the modern age. I shall not dispute all the fine and subtle points of those who argue whether there was really such a transition, whether it occurred wholly in the medieval mind or was wholly in the modern mind. That is a wonderful game for world conferences of historians. That this was a great moment of transition, I have no real doubt. One of the basic tenets of the medieval man was that in order to save himself, in order to find meaning for life and to fulfill a destiny, he must become God. He must cut himself off from the world, be filled with grace, that is with a divine energy, and rise to a divine level. He must cease to be what he was. He must become something altogether new. Man as man could no longer be endured. It was, when one looks at it closely, very much like a strand of Oriental mysticism which sees man's salvation as an escape from this world, a denial of desire and ambition, an assimilation into a nirvana, into a nothingness or an all-in-all.

Against this underling motif, the Reformation, and especially Luther himself, pitted its whole strength. Man, if he were to fulfill a destiny, if he were to be saved, must be saved as a man. Man could not, and perhaps even should not, be changed into an angel or a god. He had dignity and worth as he was. Whatever was wrong with man or his world would have to be dealt with without changing his nature, that which made him what he was. This was a tremendous affirmation of the goodness of man, of the possibilities for man.

What was wrong with man could be termed unnatural, a foreign element in his history, an intrusion of something which did not belong to man himself, an enemy. To put it bluntly, man was in a fallen state. To restore man's naturalness, to restore man's own destiny, must be what God has in mind. That God became man, is a compliment to man which restores his estimate of himself. Man is not to become something other than what he is, but he is to be restored to that which he was created to be.

The way this problem was handled by the Reformation in the light of the complexities and the strange intersecting and contradictory elements of man's experience in life is called the principle of simultaneity. We all know the good old phrase, *simul justus et peccator*. Man is at the same time, in the same moment, in the same history both just and a sinner, both saved and sinful. What was forgotten often in the Lutheran tradition which followed the Reformation was the underlying idea that this means that man is saved as he is, as he was. There is hidden in this great slogan the presupposition, the assumption, that the man who is saved, the man who is justified, the man who is a sinner, is still a man, who in the continuity of his own history is given a new destiny.

This understanding undergirds a basic commitment

to man's humanity, a commitment to the unity of mankind, a commitment to the right of every man to be human which, of course, has a great deal to say about many current subjects; about social justice, about the diversity among men, about their different ways of coming to an understanding of themselves. And it also provides not only the possibility but the necessity for men to cooperate among themselves, for every man to recognize every other man no matter what stage of development he has reached in terms of understanding himself and his destiny. A man is a man is a man, and he is a man to be identified with mankind and it is with mankind that God has chosen to deal.

This has a great deal to do with the motivating forces in every man and especially the motivations of the Christian community. If man cannot or ought not become God, then we must love him as he is and we must work with him with the potentialities which are already in him. This is, in the light of some of the things we say and do and think in the Christian community, a rather radical kind of statement. I think it is meant to be, for the Reformation said that man has the freedom to be man. Man is not only released from the drive to become God in order to be saved, but he is required to deal with other men and to deal with them with the capacities already bequeathed to them. Love your neighbor as yourself.

The Immanence of God

The time in which the Reformation was born was one in which God was being conceived of primarily in terms of his transcendence; he was above and beyond and far away. That is why in those days men built tall cathedrals with spires reaching into the sky where God was. That is why they created a priesthood set apart and gave their priests special and almost divine privileges. That is why they believed that in monasteries away from the world, in the life of contemplation whereby one could escape from this world and identify with another where God was really to be found. This was also part of the romantic age which followed. I think of the lines by Robert Browning in his poem *Pippa Passes:* "God's in his heaven, all's right with the world."

Against this kind of understanding of God, the Reformation also pitted itself and said, "God is here." He is not only there, but he is here. A few years ago Bishop J. A. T. Robinson wrote a little book while on his sick bed, called *Honest to God,* which swept the whole civilized world. Robinson had read some of the current theologians and decided that something new had been discovered—the emphasis that God is "here" and not only "there." Robinson is a very wise man and a very sincere and interesting one, but the pity was that he had not read Luther.

The idea of the immanence of God the stress on the presence of God, is a very important thrust of Reformation thinking. It is a way of thinking that rejects that kind of supernaturalism which assigns God to another place. God is always God. He remains God. He is neither to be wholly identified with the world nor wholly separated from the world. He is, to use some of Luther's most interesting and colorful language, unexpressible and inexpressible. But that inexpressibleness of God does not hide the firm conviction that he is in the world; in daily life, in public events, in all history. One can talk about the meaning of that for a very long time and misunderstand it, but the thesis is clear—God is everywhere.

A second motif is that God speaks in this world. He speaks in this world, not in some other world. And he speaks through the media of this world, through those things which are part and parcel of the nature of man's own world through water and bread and wine and books and words and acts, through the characteristics of human existence.

And thirdly, this means that Reformation theology adopts a certain kind of modesty. That is, it requires that man dare not ever be arrogant toward God, never grasp him wholly, never put him down, never enclose him, never be one step ahead of him, never somehow feel that God has come within the ken of man's power. It requires a particular kind of disposition toward God which we have encapsuled in that marvelous slogan, *faith alone*.

Man lives by faith and the Spirit and not wholly by his own wisdom. It is an approach which speaks of God being very near, but always to be learned from, always to be depended on, one who is always beyond man's own grasp. Man has been given the freedom to live with God, not just the hope that some day, in some other place, he will be with God. He is with God now, and this means a faith commitment toward God which requires responsible dealing with this world, for *this* is where God is to be found. One could almost say God is in the world to be examined. This obviously gives to man a certain kind of goal, a certain kind of hope, a certain kind of responsibility about the way he treats the world about him.

The Secularity of the World

There is a long standing opinion that Luther and the Reformation denied the use of reason. Luther once, in one of his more delightful moments called reason the devil's whore and he even gave her a name— Hulda. Luther meant only that man's reason cannot in and of itself achieve the salvation that God gives as a gift. He cannot achieve this identity that medieval man talked about by his reason. But, after all, man is man and not a cow, as Luther once said in one of his more polite expressions! The world retains its integrity and man lives in it by use of his reason.

We have at work in the history of theology a continual conversation about the relation between grace and nature. The Roman Catholic tradition in its classic style, opted for a position which presumed that grace either displaced or destroyed nature. One of the interpretations of transubstantiation is an example of that kind of underlying motif. When God comes, nature is displaced, destroyed, or transformed into something which it is not, was not before. There is no room for both grace and nature in the same place. Grace and nature are of different qualities of existence, of substance. Grace is so powerful and its purpose is so different that when it arrives, nature goes.

Against this the Reformation said that the finite *is* capable of the infinite, that God is really here and he is here in such a way that the integrity of the world has not been abandoned or changed. Man should not fear this world in itself. This means, both for the Western world and the Christian community that the freedom and the ability to deal with the world as it is is preserved. The development of modern science is not something which in and of itself has been a threat to the Christian tradition or foreign to its own hopes, or something which even in its method is unwelcome to the Christian community. For the world is to be investigated and to be loved for its own sake. One does not destroy grace by paying attention to nature and its development.

The doctrine of the real presence is a way of saying that when God comes, he enhances nature and does not displace it; for bread remains bread and wine remains wine and yet at the same time, in that strange mystery, God is given and received. And, of course, this gives a whole new sense to that thing called human responsibility.

There is a responsibility toward the world in the very understanding of the faith and man has been given a freedom to live in this world. How does one prepare for this kind of life? Is there a mission of the church which relates to this kind of responsibility? How does the church express it? From a theological standpoint one might dare say that to be religious is also to be worldly. One does not deny the secular but deals with it with a purpose.

The Reality of Evil

This is more difficult to handle, yet important, for our tradition has assumed that conflict is at the root of life. There is something called good and something called evil. There is a certain irrationality in life; there is in life a riddle. When man faces life certain questions arise which demonstrate that he does not have a full grasp of the life he has been given. There are contradictions and questions and unexplained and threatening aspects of his life which seem to express themselves over and over again in terms of conflict. The Reformation said that man does not bear the full burden of all this. Man must be freed from the devastating accusation that he is responsible for all of the conflict and for all the riddles and for the irrationality. If man is not God then neither is he the devil. Man is not "Rosemary's Baby."

If man believes that other men or that mankind is the cause of all his problems then he will in the end destroy other men to save himself. It is a devilishly subtle temptation to believe that all problems of the world are caused by the decisions of other men and that to remove those men will save the situation. But if man believes that he must fight the evil which captures *every* man, then he will work with other men to save the world. Man cannot escape despair. Only when he faces up to the realities of his enemies— of death, of suffering, of ignorance, of hopelessness— can he clearly understand his task and achieve sufficient confidence to live. The reality of evil is a necessary theme in understanding the Reformation thrust. For unless one takes evil seriously, one does not understand his mission, one does not understand what man is, one does not understand what man should do.

One of our problems has been a recurring misunderstanding of what we have called total depravity. Many have understood it to mean that man is nothing. And we have used this concept of total depravity to depress man, to destroy him in order to save him, and we have nearly equated the source of evil wholly with man. What the Reformation theology said was that total depravity is a term which should be applied as the understanding of reason was applied. Man is totally depraved in the sense that he does not have within himself, within his own nature, the power to save himself. He is too burdened with sinful inclinations, with temptations, with depravity in order to be able to escape on his own. That is a very different kind of approach. This theme has several effects.

First of all, it excludes sentimentality from religion. Religion is not a poetic exercise; it is not something which touches only on the finer points of man's sensibilities. Religion is not a romantic affair. It focuses on the realities of good and evil, and a man should not be surprised at evil or consider it an extraordinary event in history. He should be surprised only if he discovers that his life is fully harmonious and without either threats or irrationalities. To be surprised that evil exists will really only cause withdrawal from the world, lack of confidence, and increasing confusion. Man should rather take the stance of preparing himself to battle evil in order to free himself from its consequences.

The second effect is that this kind of understanding develops virile people, people who are interested in accomplishment, who desire to ally themselves with the forces of good which shape history, who believe they have a mission which relates to things as they really are and who accept the possibility of change. They do not succumb to the irrationalities of life. They are redeemed for a purpose.

And it means, thirdly, that man dealing with realities, with the world as it is, does so with the understanding that this dealing requires moral judgment. The world is not a neutral entity. It is not simply protons and electrons put together in all kinds of interesting designs which result in a machine in which man lives as a robot. The world is alive with movement, with conflict, and with accomplishment, and it requires more than an objective "looking on." It requires more than serene analysis or eloquence. It requires engagement. I don't know of any better single reason for our existence or for the mission of the church.

The Power of the Future

The basis for life, says the Reformation, is not a full comprehension of the ultimate, but a hope for the future, a confidence in the future victory of God for mankind, a faith in a destiny which has been given and which belongs, by virtue of its gifts, to man. One of the basic categories of the Reformation heritage is the understanding of the movement of history which has an end, which has a purpose, already anticipated in a past historical event which we call Jesus Christ. And as simple as that sounds, and as perhaps as vague as it sounds, it is a statement which has great consequences for what a man thinks and does and is. For the future is viewed not as a simple ascending staircase, or as some kind of void, but as hope. Man can shake this history. Future history does depend on man, but does not depend on man for its finality, a very important difference. Man can understand that he has a responsibility for the future, but he does not carry the burden for its finality, for that belongs to one we trust and that finality has already been guaranteed by him.

New-found discoveries about the sources of our faith and perhaps the dying of some old superstitions have not shaken the fundamental orientation of the Reformation communities in which we live. Men still live for the future. I think that to a certain extent the existentialists are right in saying that the basic threat to every man is his fear of nonexistence, is his fear of that future moment when he may no longer be. The Reformation deals with this and speaks to it. There is a pulling in every man, a pulling toward that which is not yet, toward that future where God waits. For God is not only here and there, but he is also in the future and there is nothing which speaks more vibrantly to the modern man, to the despair and to the human dimensions of this generation than that gospel.

For I think this generation is lost in the conflict between the two understandings and meanings we discussed in an earlier chapter. The first of these we called radical existentialism. This is the idea that reality belongs only within man, that man only knows truth or knows the world when he knows himself. The second and opposite view is analytic philosophy which believes that man can only discover truth in the world—I know myself when I know the world. This is the basis for the theories of truth in the scientific method. Being caught between these two ideas which this culture places before him as the choice he must make, man finds no way out, and so he lives in what we call a secular age. This is the insidious and demonic lie that there is only man and he must deal with everything himself and there is no real future.

Is Reformation theology viable for the modern man? If you have missed the point, I have said yes. Does it speak to man's condition as he is in this generation? I say yes. Does it leave us free for hope? The answer is yes. And does it suggest itself as a basis for the mission of the church whereby the church as a Christian community explores the frontiers and engages in a world God not only has given us in which to live, but one which he has given us to serve? The answer is yes.